PRAYER:
The Integration of Faith and Life

BERNARD HÄRING
PRAYER:
The Integration of Faith and Life

FIDES PUBLISHERS, INC.
NOTRE DAME, INDIANA

© 1975: Fides Publishers, Inc.
        Notre Dame, Indiana 46556

Nihil obstat: G. E. Roberts
Imprimatur: Charles Grant, Bishop of Northampton

ISBN: 0-8190-0609-2 Cloth
      0-8190-0611-4 Paper

To the memory of my dear parents
who first communicated to me
the gladdening news
and joy in prayer

CONTENTS

ACKNOWLEDGEMENT

I thank all those who, in the past years, have helped me to understand better what prayer is and how much strength and life it grants to us. The contact with various 'houses of prayer' has given me much inspiration.

I thank, above all, Mrs Josephine Ryan, who again has offered her generous help in typing and editing the text of this book.

PREFACE

The following pages are the fruit of many shared meditations with diverse groups of persons in various countries, especially in houses of prayer and schools of faith.

In the present crisis of faith it is not enough to tell people to 'pray ... pray hard'. They want, above all, to know what genuine prayer is, and how they can pray in a way that does not separate faith from life but brings faith into their daily life and brings all their life home to God.

Prayer is loving knowledge of God, a constant longing to know him in order to love him, and to know his design for us in order to serve him better. So, we are to meditate here on the names of Jesus, in such a way that the knowledge of our Lord becomes the programme of our life. Thus prayer is theology and all theology becomes prayer.

Prayer is attention to God's coming into our life, a recognition of the grace of the present hour, and unfailing vigilance for the Lord's calling. It is the most personal and most personalizing event in human life. Nothing brings people closer together in oneness, brotherhood and solidarity than to call the one God 'Our Father', to know Christ as the 'man for all mankind', and to rely on the grace of the Holy Spirit who, through his manifold gifts, is building up the unity of the whole human race.

The future of the Church, and equally of mankind, depends on that integration which true prayer-life promotes and expresses. The Church therefore, needs schools of prayer — houses of prayer — which are at the same time schools of faith and of life according to faith.

PRAYER:
THE INTEGRATION OF FAITH AND LIFE

Chapter 1

KNOWING THE NAME OF THE LORD
AND PRAYING IN HIS NAME

In his most solemn prayer Jesus said, 'This is eternal life: to know you who alone are true God, and Jesus Christ whom you have sent. I have made your name known to those whom you gave me out of the world. Now they know that all your gifts come to me from you' (Jn 17:3-7).

Our life is authentically Christian to the extent that we know Christ and listen to his word with a readiness to respond with our whole being. Christian life needs prayer: the integration of faith and life. In its full meaning, prayer is joyous acceptance of life's greatest gift, the Lord's friendship, and the return of the gift of one's self to God in the service of one's fellowmen.

When God speaks to us, inviting us to respond to him and to rejoice in him, his word is a manifestation of himself and of his name. Christ has assigned great importance to the revelation of the name of God, the name 'Father', and to prayer in his own name. To understand the significance of the names of God and the names of the One whom he has sent us, we have to remember what a name meant in Hebrew culture.

When a child was born, all the members of the family with friends and neighbours, meditated together about the name that should be given to this child. The name was meant as the expression of a mystery, as a programme of life, as a message and appeal. When the friends of Elizabeth and Zechariah had gathered to celebrate God's gift of a son to those who had desired him with such great faith and hope, they came to the conclusion that he should be given the name of his father, Zechariah. But the father's response was, 'No; his name is John', which means 'God has shown mercy'. The life of John the Baptist was authentic because he remained faithful to the programme signified by his name. By word and witnessing life, he made known to many that God is merciful love.

In many African cultures it is still a great event to find the most appropriate name for a child. For these people it does not make sense to give a name in baptism which does not proclaim to them a meaning.

I once asked a sympathetic catechist in Chad, Central Africa, about his name and its meaning. He answered immediately, 'Abandoned and driven into the desert'. And he explained, 'I was my mother's only comfort when she was abandoned and driven away by my father who submitted to that cruel rule for baptism which required, in polygamist cultures, that a man's second wife must be dismissed. My father made the decision to divorce my mother with a bleeding heart. He did not know that she was pregnant. My name is a call to compassion and to gratitude because my mother raised me in the midst of great difficulties'.

Another of my good African friends has the name, 'There is still hope'. His mother had lost a number of children, and when he was born, all the friends decided that, for him, this was the most appropriate name.

Mohammedans have a kind of rosary which is an invocation of the various names of God. It can become a very profound meditation about what they know of God, of his wisdom, his might and mercy. To recite the rosary of the names of God means, for them, to honour God, his name, and the attributes revealed by him throughout history. It is an expression of trust in God and of growth in knowledge of his design. This old tradition has been the source of many beautiful prayers among both Mohammedans and Christians. I quote, from memory, one from the Egyptian Mohammedans which seems most characteristic:

'Blessed be the Most High. He says to his servants: "Seek me and you shall find me.

I am the Almighty who calls everything into being: seek me and you shall find me.

I am the judge: seek me with a humble heart and you shall find me.

I am the giver of all good gifts, who gives lavishly the signs of his love: seek me and you shall find me.

I am the One who forgives; trust in me. Seek me and you shall find me.

I am strength for all men; your refuge I am. Seek me and you shall find me.

I am the all-wise God who knows how to protect you against all enemies, and to guide you: seek me and you shall find me.

I am the advocate of widows and orphans, of all who seek me sincerely: seek me and you shall find me.

I am the One who listens to those who beseech me. I hear the prayers of my servants: seek me and you shall find me.

If you adore me while you implore my help, I am near to you: seek me and you shall find me.

Do you not know that I am closer to you than the beating of your heart? Seek me and you shall find me".'

We Christians have various prayers similar to this appealing prayer of the Mohammedans. One is the litany of the names of Jesus. In the following meditations, I do not follow all the beautiful invocations of this litany, but choose those biblical names of Jesus which can communicate to men of today the most vital knowledge of God and the most concrete and challenging programme of Jesus' life.

To pray in the name of Jesus, it is important to know the meaning of his name and of all the other names which attest to his goodness, his fidelity, his mercy and his loving presence among us.

If we know the name of Jesus, then we know also the name of God the Father, whom Christ has revealed to us.

✦ O God and Father, you have made glorious your name in your Son, Jesus Christ. Let us pray with all our life, 'Hallowed, honoured, adored and loved be your name by all your children, united in your beloved Son, gathered by the one Spirit. This we ask in the name of Jesus.

1. *Jesus*

'Jesus' (Joshua) means 'God is our salvation'.

God is saving love and the all-powerful benefactor for those who call upon his name. To know and to call upon the name of Jesus is, above all, an expression of our trust in him. It is also our humble avowal that we need him and therefore humbly and trustfully beg him to hear us.

In Russia, the 'Jesus prayer' is regarded as the epitome of Christian prayer. It follows the pattern of the blind man of Jericho, Bartimeus, the beggar by the roadside who, when he heard that Jesus was passing by, cried out to him, 'Jesus, Son of David, have pity on me' (Mk 10:47). Some in the crowd accompanying Jesus scolded him, told him to be quiet; but he shouted all the louder, 'Jesus, Son of David, have pity on me!' With sure intuition, he knew that only this man could restore sight to his eyes.

We, too, know the name of Jesus and can call upon him with perfect trust if all our daily life expresses the profound consciousness that Christ alone is the light that illumines us and the way of our salvation. If we know that, then we also know that the abiding reality and the highest values are gratuitous gifts of God, and that those who call upon his name receive these gifts. This is salvation.

When we call upon the name of Jesus, we are renouncing all false trust in ourselves. Those who put their trust in themselves and in the works of their hands — those things made by the technical men — will never come to know truly the name of Jesus. They will ever echo the absurd prayer of the cock who, day by day, from the dunghill that symbolizes the misery of our vanity, crows, 'Lord, I am your servant; but never forget, it is I who make the sun rise!'

Only in trustful and persevering prayer do we come gradually to the full knowledge of the name of Jesus, and thus, to the experience of that love of which St Paul says, 'There is no limit to its trust' (1 Cor 13:3). And if we unite with others in calling upon the name of Jesus, the Saviour of all, then we hope for each other, encourage each other, give credit to each other, respect and love each other.

✝ O Jesus, to you I turn my eyes and my heart. You are the life of my life, and my light. Free me from foolish trust in my own strength and ability. Let me trust in you and in you alone, because you are our salvation, our joy and beatitude. Give me that wholesome trust in my own capacities which is grounded only in gratitude and in appreciation of the good that is in others. You are our only saviour; give us strength.

Lord, open my eyes that I may see the limits of my own abilities, and give me courage to accept these limits, so that I may become ever more aware that you alone are my strength.

2. *Christ: the Anointed*

We often end our prayers with the words, 'in the name of Jesus Christ'. Jesus is the Christ, the Messiah whom the forefathers expected, anointed by the Holy Spirit. He is our saviour.

In Christ, the eternal Word of the Father lives in absolute fullness, as gift from the Father and as Word that is total response to the Father in that mutual dialogue and mutual self-bestowal which is the Holy Spirit, the total, joyous gift of self.

The human nature of Jesus, too, united with the Word, is anointed with the oil of gladness so that, though he makes himself the lowly servant, he is filled with joy and is ever the source of joy. By the power of the Spirit he is sent to bring us gladdening news.

United with the Father in the Holy Spirit, Christ radiates joy and peace to all who venerate and call upon his name. And for all who seek their delight and their salvation in him alone, Jesus Christ is the Lord.

We adore and honour the name of Christ whenever we hear the gladdening news with open hearts and accept his beatitudes as gifts and as direction for our lives. If we know the name of Christ, we are ready to travel the road that leads to him, the source and centre of our joy.

✝ O Christ, anointed by the Father in the power of the Spirit, send us your Holy Spirit to purify us and to open our hearts and minds to your joy. Free us from all wrong expectations and desires that lead us to seek joy where it will not be found.

Free us, O Lord, from the illusions that mislead us, and give us courage to renounce distractions and to overcome our dissipations. Help us to receive your word, gratefully to treasure it in our hearts and to rejoice in it, so that we too may be messengers of joy and peace for our brothers and sisters.

3. Christ, the Poor One, sent by the Spirit

We know the spirit of people by the ideals and tasks to which they dedicate themselves. The Spirit that rests upon

Christ and sends him is made known to us by his whole life and, above all, by his death, his readiness to give himself totally for the salvation of his fellowmen. 'And the Spirit of the Lord shall rest upon him, the Spirit of wisdom and of understanding, the Spirit of counsel and of fortitude, the Spirit of knowledge and of the fear of the Lord. . . The earth shall be filled with the knowledge of the Lord, as the waters cover the sea' (Is 11: 2-9).

In everything Christ does, he is guided by the Spirit. The Spirit leads him into the desert where he lives 'on every word that comes from the mouth of God'. The Spirit comes visibly upon him in his baptism in the Jordan where he shows his readiness to bear the burden of all men and to be the brother of all people. It is by the power of the Holy Spirit that Jesus drives out evil spirits and cures the sick. Through the power of the Spirit he is the Poor One, the Blessed who brings the kingdom of God.

When Jesus speaks for the first time in the synagogue in his own town of Nazareth, he reads from the second Isaiah the great canticle about the servant messiah: 'The Spirit of the Lord is upon me because he has anointed me to announce good news to the poor; he has sent me to proclaim release for prisoners, recovery of sight to the blind, freedom to the broken victims, and to proclaim the year of the Lord's favour' (Lk 4: 18-19).

For Christ, the joy of the Spirit is the strength to dedicate himself to the poor, the rejected, the dispossessed, and all who are slaves of a selfish world.

In his high-priestly prayer, Christ describes himself as 'the Anointed': 'For them I have consecrated myself, that they too may be consecrated in truth' (Jn 17: 19). So will all those who welcome Christ and entrust themselves to his Spirit be consecrated, anointed with the oil of gladness, and be given strength to be messengers of peace, liberation and reconciliation.

Consecration in truth demands a rigorous insistence upon what is authentic. It totally contradicts, for instance, any form of legalism that is more concerned with ritual and canonical validity than with Christian authenticity. Those who, with Christ the Anointed, are anointed by the Spirit, will receive God's gifts with such gratitude that they are enabled to live for the common good, using the grace of each hour.

✝ We pray, O Lord, in your name 'Christ-the Anointed', that you send us your Spirit to consecrate us in truth as your true disciples. Free us from selfishness and narrowness, from vanity, distractions and pride, so that we may become ever more able to receive the beatitudes promised to those who live with you and are docile to your Spirit.

Grant us that holy joy in you that gives us the strength to offer ourselves, for the glory of the Father, to all those who need us, and especially those who need from us an authentic word and action.

4. *Christ, the Servant*

Christ is announced as 'The Servant of the Lord' in the great poems of the second Isaiah. 'Here is my servant whom I uphold, my chosen one in whom I am pleased; upon whom I have put my spirit: he shall bring forth justice to the nations. He shall not cry out, not shout, not make his voice heard in the street. The bruised reed he shall not break and the smouldering wick he shall not quench' (Is 42: 1-3).

As Christians, all our life should acknowledge the name 'Servant-Messiah', which means that united with Christ we learn from his total humility and total readiness to bear the burden of mankind and to renounce all earthly power.

Christ the Servant was destined to be a sign that would be rejected. Many in Israel stood or fell because of him, and thus 'the secret thoughts of many hearts have been laid bare' (cf. Lk 2: 34-35). The whole public life of Jesus up to his death itself is a history of tension between two different kinds of messianic expectations. Those who rejected him had been waiting for a national hero, a power-messiah. Even the disciples of Christ had been affected by this erroneous hope; but all except Judas Iscariot were finally converted to Christ the Servant.

Mary, the mother of the Lord, and the *anawim* — the humble people in the country — welcomed Christ because they expected a servant-messiah, a humble and gentle servant of God and of man.

The Church, from the beginning, through the Constantinian era and up to our own time, has lived with this historic tension between the saints who, with their whole life, adore Christ the Servant, and those who arrogate to themselves direct or indirect power over the temporal sphere in a spirit devoid of humility and simplicity. It is not possible to pray in the name of Jesus Christ the Servant unless we want to join our life totally with his life in the service of God, as humble and generous servants of the common good.

Christ is the Lord, the source of joy for all people. By the power of the Spirit he took the burden of our sins upon himself: 'Yet it was our infirmities that he bore, our sufferings that he endured, while we thought of him as stricken, as one smitten by God and afflicted. But he was pierced for our offences, crushed for our sins. Upon him was the chastisement that makes us whole. By his stripes we were healed' (Is 53:4-6).

✝ In the name of Christ the Servant, we praise you, Father, Lord of heaven and earth, for having fully revealed to your humble servant Jesus, your Son and our brother, your secrets that remain hidden from the wise and arrogant.

He is your beloved servant who made himself servant to all; and for this reason you have made him Lord over all your people and over all things. You have given him a name above all names.

Christ, your Servant, is our beatitude, the beatitude of all who are humble in a new spirit, as he was, and who stand before you as beggars and receive your gifts gratefully in order to serve our brothers and sisters. Christ, your Servant, is the reconciliation and peace, the source of blessedness for all who are gentle and compassionate messengers of peace.

Send forth your Spirit, Lord, that we too, anointed by the same Spirit which led Christ to give himself as ransom for the salvation of the world, may find the courage and endurance to serve our neighbour. Let our concern be not so much to be understood as to understand, not so much to be the object of love and admiration as to love those who are most in need of it. Help us to become free servants of all, never seeking to impress, manipulate or condition anyone.

Father, we know that if we ask for this gift in the name of your son Jesus, your Servant, you will always be with us. We pray to you today, Father, that our prayer may be sincere, that we may truly long for this great gift, and then be ready to accept the humiliations and all those unexpected and undesired experiences in life that make us similar to your Son and Servant, Jesus Christ.

5. *The New Israel*

The whole life of Mary, 'daughter of Sion', sings about the New Israel: 'God is with Israel, his servant' (Lk 1: 56).

Who is this servant called Israel? It is the chosen people, among whom Mary is the fairest daughter. Above all, it is her Son, in whom all the expectations of Israel are fulfilled. It is also all those who, with Mary the handmaid, follow Christ as servants and thus manifest the redemption wrought by 'the New Israel, the Servant'.

Literally, 'Israel' means 'one who has struggled with God' (Gen 32: 21-31). It was the name given to Jacob, forefather of the twelve tribes, as a more significant name after he had struggled with God and experienced the mystery of God's holiness. He was forever marked with a sign of suffering, but at the same time he had been forcefully attracted by God, the source of all blessing: 'I shall not let you go until you have blessed me' (Gen 32:27).

Jesus, the New Israel, also endured the struggle, the frightening experience of sinful mankind faced with the all-holy God: 'My God, my God, why have you forsaken me?' (Mk 15:34). And in that struggle he reveals the victory of trust, the final response to the love of the Father drawing him: 'Father, into your hands I commit my spirit' (Lk 23:46). In this victorious struggle with the Father, in this final pleading for mercy for all the forsaken, and in absolute trust in the Father's compassion, the full meaning of the name 'Israel' applies to Jesus.

In the great messianic prophecies of the second Isaiah, God's language is most tender when he foretells the coming of Israel his Servant in the fullness of time. 'But you Israel, my servant, offspring of Abraham my friend: you whom I have taken from the ends of the earth and summoned from its far-off places; you whom I have called my servant, whom I have chosen and will not cast out: fear not, I am with you' (Is 41:8-10). 'Remember this, O Jacob, you, O Israel who are my servant: I have formed you to be a servant to me. O Israel, by me you shall never be forgotten' (Is 44:21).

All the names of Jesus reveal various aspects of the same mystery, the mystery of redemption, of suffering, of the victory of love and trust, of humility and glory, of the fear of the Lord and of joy in him. The names 'Israel' and 'Servant' relate to the whole history of Israel from the time of the old and new covenants to the present day when the Church of the New Israel, which should be experiencing all the blessings given to Israel, has to undergo again and again Jacob's painful struggle — indeed the struggle of Christ himself — as it faces the all-holy God who exalts the humble and puts to rout the arrogant.

Jacob (Israel) and his descendants were chosen by God from nothingness to be his people, the people of the covenant. They had the guarantee of God's blessing as long as they would remain faithful servants of the one God, not seeking earthly power among the nations, but glorifying the name of God and making him and his undeserved love known to all nations.

But all too often in its history, Israel forgot the struggle of the forefather Jacob, and sought worldly power and even misused religion for self-aggrandizement. It began to interpret wealth and success as a sign of its being chosen, forgetting that all this comes from God and can be a blessing only if it is used for the benefit of all men and all nations. Israel's religious mission became darkened and was finally betrayed when the powerful and privileged class of Judah refused to receive Christ, the Servant, the New Israel.

No part or fraction of the Christian Church has any right to look with contempt on the Israelites because of all this. Christianity has to repent even more than Israel for having sacralized unholy wars, for having looked for direct power over all earthly affairs, and for having too often forgotten and even betrayed the New Israel, Jesus Christ, the Servant of God and of mankind.

We, the sons and daughters of the Church, can sing the Magnificat of Mary, the humble handmaid, and can call upon us the blessing of the name 'Israel the Servant' to the extent that we avoid the selfishness and the personal and group power struggles that we find in the history of Israel and Judah and in the history of our Church. If we struggle with God in the same spirit of gentleness, non-violence, compassion and humility as that of Christ, then we shall have forever a share in the beatitude of Christ, foreshadowed by the blessing given to Jacob. And this will be a blessing for all nations and for all men and women.

✝ O Jesus, son of David, Israel the Servant, have mercy on us all; make us humble and gentle, that we may gain the whole earth to faith in you. Convert us to you: convert us all,

Christians, Jews and Mohammedans to the One God, your Father and our Father.

Make us fully aware that our faith — our belonging to your Church — is your gratuitous gift in which we can rejoice only when we accept it as a challenge to serve you in our brothers and sisters. Help us to rely on you, to praise and thank you, and to follow you, the New Israel, the Servant of God and of all his people.

O Mary, daughter of Sion, because of your Son and you, we love your people, who gave us you and your gentle husband Joseph. We shall not forget that this same people gave to the world many saints and martyrs, and many faithful Israelites like Nathaniel. Pray for us, that our life may proclaim your Son, the New Israel, and that God may make us humble, since he wants to reveal himself to the single-hearted and the little ones. If we follow, with you, Christ the Servant, then we shall have eternal life in us and grow in the knowledge of God the Father and of his Son, Jesus Christ.

6. *The Way, the Truth and the Life*

Thomas said, 'Lord, we do not know where you are going. How can we know the way?' Jesus answered, 'I am the way, the truth and the life; no one comes to the Father but through me. If you really knew me, you would know my Father also. Henceforth you do know him, for you have seen him' (Jn 14: 5-7).

Jesus comes from the Father and returns to him in order to show us the way to the Father. No one can come to the Father and know him except those to whom the Son reveals him. Jesus alone is truly the Sacrament, the visible and effective sign of the Father and his love: 'Whoever has seen me has seen the Father' (Jn 14: 9).

Jesus did not come for his own sake or to please himself but to free us from alienation and slavery and to bring us home to the Father. He is the Way because he is the Truth and the Life, the living Word of the Father. What he communicates to us is not abstract ideas or ideologies but the most concrete reality: that God is love and calls all men to be sharers of his life and love.

Christ is not a word like other words. He is the one Word in whom the Father speaks all his wisdom, all his love, and his loving design for man. And Christ, Son of the Father, is the Word that breathes love and becomes man in order to share with us that knowledge of the Father and love for the Father which make us able to love each other with his own love, and thus to honour the Father's name.

We begin to pray in the name of Jesus, the Way and the Truth, when we stop discussing his way and his truth only in terms of abstract ideas, or idle speculations, or by hunting for heresies on behalf of man-made formulations which can be conditioned and abused. We honour his name when we are seeking, with all our heart and mind, that truth which gives life and enables us to become witnesses to that love which has created and redeemed us.

Christ is that truth which is life, which can never be found through debate and discussion. He reveals himself only to those who are ready to hear his word, to treasure it in their hearts, and to put it into practice, in order to bear fruit in love and justice for the life of the world. Christ is that truth which can never be grasped by the proud and arrogant but only by those who understand and humbly acknowledge the gratuitous nature of revelation.

Christ is, at the same time, our Truth and our Life, since he truthfully reveals to us the name of the Father by making himself the brother of all, calling all of us to blood-brotherhood by shedding his blood, the blood of the new and everlasting covenant. By his word and his life, Christ teaches us that we cannot know the invisible God and himself, the Father's image, unless we begin to love our brothers and try to love them as he loved us. He shares his life and his death with us, that we too may become images of the Father who loves all his children and wants them to have life, and everlasting life, through his Spirit.

Christ does not reveal himself and the Father to those who fight for a sterile orthodoxy which they reduce to words and formulas without committing themselves to a life according to that ultimate truth which allows no escapism. In him, truth and life coincide. He himself, who has so perfectly fulfilled the law of love, of mercy and of justice, is the incarnate orthodoxy.

Christianity — Christian faith — is not an ideology; it is a life with Christ. It is the history of God and man: being on the road with Christ who comes from the Father and wants to bring us all together and lead us home to the blessed life with the Triune God.

✠ Christ, Son of the living God, son of David, have mercy on me and heal me of my blindness. Let your Holy Spirit come upon me, so that with a pure heart I may know you who are my life and the truth that saves me.

Have mercy on me, fool that I am, who day after day collect a thousand useless pieces of news, and hour after hour allow the superficial images of television, magazines and the latest paperback to shape me. Grant that I may turn my eyes and my heart to you, and in all things and all events be reminded of your presence. You are the Way that leads us through shared sufferings and joys, through shared hope and anguish, to the one Father. Make us one, make us holy.

O Lord, living Sacrament of the invisible Father, grant that it may always be the first purpose and greatest longing of my life to know you in order to know the Father and to know better how to love my brothers and sisters. Give me, O Lord, courage to seek you and your loving word above all things, in order to act on it. And give me a humble heart and the strength to recognize and to confess my sins whenever I have not acted upon the truth which you have revealed to my conscience.

7. Christ, the Covenant

The key word of the whole Old Testament is *berit*: covenant. The covenant is an undeserved gift which gives meaning and energy to the law and to every event. The Israelites can rejoice in the law of the Lord because it is an expression of their covenant with God and helps them to live within it.

It is unthinkable that this great prophetic vision of the covenant would suddenly disappear in the New Testament. On the contrary, it is not only an essential idea but it is the ful-filled promise, the life-giving reality in Jesus Christ. All that the Old Testament says about the covenant of God with man is a promise and preparation for what becomes full truth in Christ who is the Covenant. The promised servant of God is the covenant in person: 'I, the Lord have called you in justice, and taken you by the hand; I formed you and set you as a covenant of the people, a light for the nations' (Is 42:6).

Christ is the saving, living law for our life because he is the incarnate, saving solidarity. 'He shall instruct us in his ways and we shall walk in his paths; for the law shall come forth from Sion, and the word of the Lord from Jerusalem' (Is 2:3).

In his famous book, *Dialogue With Tryphon*, Justin, one of the great Christian thinkers of the first half of the second century, honours Christ with the name, 'The Law and The Covenant'. Christ is our life-giving law, our way, by being the Incarnate Covenant. The message and way of salvation written in the blood of the new and everlasting covenant is incarnate solidarity: the message is that One lived and died for all, so that no one should ever live for himself alone but for Christ and with Christ for his brothers and sisters. All that gives meaning to our life is that we should make our choice firmly and truthfully for Christ, the saving covenant, saving solidarity, and thus be freed from the solidarity of perdition and death.

It is surprising that individualism could grow so strong that devotion, spirituality and theology could almost completely forget this essential name, Christ the Covenant. Perhaps no other name of Christ is more important for our prayer and as a programme for our lives.

Christ is the Covenant, since he is one with the Father and one with us. 'O Father, most holy: protect them with your name which you have given me: that they may be one, even as we are one... I pray also for those who will believe in me through their witnessing word, so that all may be one, as you, Father, are in me and I in you; that they also may be one in us, that the world may believe that you have sent me' (Jn 17: 11-21).

We could translate that scholastic expression 'hypostatic union' and speak also of 'hypostatic covenant.' Christ's oneness with the Father cannot be severed from his oneness with all mankind. His basic self-revelation, 'I am in the Father and the Father in me' is followed by that other not less important statement, 'I in you and you in me'. Almost two hundred times we may turn, in the epistles of St Paul and in the gospel of St John, to the basic truth that we have life in Christ and are exhorted to live in Christ. This means, above all, that we are called to live with him who is one with the Father and who is the saving solidarity for all sons and daughters of the Father. The name of Jesus Christ as covenant is happily translated by Dietrich Bonhoeffer as 'the man for others', since the covenant is the great gift and call to liberating solidarity in justice, peace, kindness, gentleness, and love.

Christ is the only perfect monotheist. His whole life and his death is revelation of the one Father, who calls all mankind to unity. Christ's death seals his claim to be the Son, since he honours the one Father by being the brother of all, to the point of blood-brotherhood. His resurrection is the final seal of the new covenant given by the Father through the power of the Spirit. The Father has glorified him as Lord of all because he wanted to be the servant and brother of all.

In the Old Testament, the sign and seal of belonging to the covenant was circumcision. In the New Testament, the great signs of our sharing in the covenant are baptism and the Eucharist. Together with the other sacraments, they are signs of our belonging to Christ, the saving Covenant.

By his baptism, Christ reveals himself to the world as the Covenant. He does not come to John the Baptist to receive a baptism apart from others, but comes 'during a general baptism' (Lk 3:21). Thus he manifests that he is the Lamb of God who takes upon himself the sin-burden of all mankind. In order to free and to heal all men, he who is without sin inserts himself into mankind. Christ is ready to suffer because of man's solidarity in sinfulness, in oppression, in manipulation, and in blindness. By sharing the collective burden that oppresses sinful mankind, he becomes the Way that leads to a new freedom through solidarity in him, the saving Covenant.

He is solemnly acknowledged by the Father as the 'beloved Son' when, through baptism, he manifests his firm purpose to fulfil the new justice by putting himself totally at the service of all people. This is the new justice of which Jesus speaks when John the Baptist tries to refuse him baptism with the protest, 'I should be baptized by you; yet you come to me'. Jesus answers, 'Let it be this way for now; for by doing this we shall fulfil all of God's justice' (Mt 3:14-15).

By the blood of the new and everlasting covenant, Christ gives thanks and praise to the Father of all humankind. His thanksgiving for the insertion of his human nature into the dignity of the Son is translated into solidarity with the whole of creation. His second baptism, in his blood, made possible by the power of the Holy Spirit, completes what is symbolized by the ritual baptism in the Jordan. 'Jesus Christ is he who comes through water and blood: not in water alone but in water and in blood; and it is the Spirit who testifies to this, the Spirit who is truth. Thus there are three that testify: the Spirit and the water and the blood. These three are of one accord' (1 Jn 5:6-7).

Our baptism inserts us into Jesus Christ, and we live

according to baptism if, by allowing his Spirit to free us from selfishness, we involve ourselves in his liberating love. So if, in the creed, we say 'we believe in one baptism', we profess the great mystery of Christ the Covenant, and we renew our vows to live with him, for him and through him, in loving service of our fellowmen.

Christ is the Covenant, and thus the new law. In practice, this means that we cannot have a share in him, the Covenant, unless we follow him as servant in his saving and redeeming solidarity with mankind. Only by bearing one another's burdens and helping one another on the road to salvation, by preparing a healthier environment, a divine *milieu*, do we fulfil the law of Christ (cf. Gal 6: 2).

✝ Christ, you who are the Covenant, Son of the living God, son of man, keep us from the selfishness that makes us accessories to mankind's collective ruin. You who have received for us baptism in water and in blood, send us your Spirit, that we may be able to live according to the law of the new and everlasting covenant, to the praise of the one Father and in unwavering commitment to work for a more just, more humane, more brotherly and thus more redeemed world.

Jesus Christ, with your blood you have revealed yourself as the new and everlasting covenant, since you did not come to be served but to serve and to offer yourself as ransom for all. Grant that, by our life-blood, we may bring into our world, our *milieu*, the same saving law, in readiness to renounce everything that could damage the salvation of our brothers.

Renew in us, O Lord, the grace of baptism, so that we can celebrate the Eucharist as the great sign of unity, charity, peace and justice, and render thanks with you to the Father who gave us, in you, the saving Covenant.

Lord and Father of Jesus Christ, make us holy, make us one, that the world may believe that there is salvation in your only begotten Son, who took the flesh of our world and became brother of all your people.

8. *Jesus, the Dialogue*

Christ is the Dialogue incarnate. The eternal Word of the Father reveals himself as the perfect expression of the love and wisdom of his Father, for himself and for all who are to be created and renewed in him, the Lord.

The human nature of Christ is totally united with the eternal Word, and lives in utter harmony with and through the Word that comes from the Father. The hypostatic union between the eternal Son of the Father and the human nature of Jesus is an absolutely gratuitous gift to human nature. Therefore the Word is received in absolute humility. Jesus listens to the Father in awareness of the gratuity of his being and his mission. Thus his whole life becomes total response to the Father in the name of mankind.

Dialogue means, above all, readiness and capacity to listen. Rightly, then, one of the names of Jesus is, 'The One Who Listens'. 'The Lord God has given me a disciple's tongue, that I might know how to speak to the weary. Morning after morning, he opens my ear, that I may listen' (Is 50:4).

The marvellous creativity, spontaneity and initiative of Jesus, true man, have their source in his total openness to the Word that comes from the Father and, at the same time, openness to the word that comes from brothers and sisters. Because his whole life respects the initiative of the Father and the gift of the Holy Spirit, he knows how to use to the full the grace of every hour prepared by the Father.

The Servant of God listens to the Father by giving all his loving attention to the cry of his suffering brothers and sisters. His intimacy with the Father brings him closest to all men, and in his compassionate love he understands them better than they understand themselves. He listens to them in total readiness to respond, and his answering word is therefore concrete and meets them in the depths of their being.

Our capacity to pray — that is, to listen to God and respond to him with our whole being — increases when we listen with open ears and hearts to the needs of our fellowmen and allow them to disturb us, to appeal to our generosity. We listen not only to their spoken words, but with the heart of a father, a mother, a brother, a physician, we listen to what they try to communicate. We truly want to understand them. But we should know also that our capacity to understand our fellowmen's needs, their dignity and their desire to be respected and loved, increases when we listen to the word of God and ponder our response before him.

We are with Christ and Christ abides with us when we are listening to others, not to judge them but to heal and to help them. In his prayer, the great sufferer, Job, says some beautiful but also some senseless things. God, however, responds with kindness to the sincerity of his whole behaviour and his whole outcry. He knows the hidden intentions of Job's heart. Our way of meeting our fellowmen should be similar. Our neighbour's bitter or aggressive word can often call our attention to the wounds and sufferings of his heart and mind. Then we find the right response: patient, gentle, full of respect and kindness.

We truly praise the name of Jesus, the Dialogue, the Listener, if we are learning an attitude of openness and do not forget the Holy Spirit. Christ shows himself to be the attentive listener by his total response to the Father. It is not he who determines the great moments of decision; he respects the initiative of the Father and waits for the hour prepared by him. 'Thy will, not mine be done'.

The lack of readiness to listen to the Spirit is the cause of today's alienation in religion and prayer. Man makes his own discourse before God instead of receiving God's word and responding to it. True prayer is based on total respect for God's own initiative, for his gifts, his message, and for the hour of joy or suffering, as he has prepared it.

In the Talmud of Babylon we find a beautiful page of

spirituality, truthful and faithful to the Bible. There we learn about a rabbi who had been meeting all the great teachers of Israel, but none of them could give an answer to his problem. He therefore made a long and dangerous journey to see the most famous of all the rabbis. To him he complained, 'I have a question which no one has answered up to now'. The great rabbi asked, 'What is it?' And then we hear a question that might not be too alien to us: 'How do I get God to do my will?' The wise teacher responded, 'Only the spirit of the Lord can give us the answer. It is he who teaches us to seek our repose in him, to abandon ourselves to his loving design, and thus, in everything he sends us and tells us to do, we find ourselves, the best of our own will.'

In the spirituality of Alphonsus of Liguori, the great teacher of prayer, we find two complementary essential ideas: first, liberation from one's own selfish desires, and second, conformity with the will of God. To gain distance from our own desire is always a necessary condition for finding our true self and permitting the Holy Spirit to free us from narrowness and arbitrariness. The goal is always conformity to the loving will of God.

When we pray to Christ, the Listener, therefore, we eliminate all self-interest. We fix our attention wholly on God's love, his gifts, and the needs of our brothers and sisters, so that we shall act in joyous trust that everything which God sends us is truly the right thing for us to accept and to respond to. Without this basic preparation for our response, listening will not suffice. In the sermon on the mount, Christ teaches us that only the one who listens to his word, treasures it, and acts according to it, is his true disciple.

A strange theology has separated the Church into two classes, 'the teaching church' and 'the learning church', and in practice this has come to mean 'the commanding church' and 'the church that has to obey'. The right concept of the Church, however, is the one Church that follows Christ the Listener. This means that those who are best in listening and learning are our most reliable teachers. Those who occupy teaching offices in the Church should be the people best fitted to gather the experiences and reflections and to understand the joys and sorrows, the hopes and anguish of mankind, and to promote dialogue and discernment. The effective and prophetic word can be said only by those who are outstanding listeners.

Saint Francis of Assisi, a humble, uncomplicated man, was a greater teacher and spiritual authority in the Church of his time than the powerful Pope Innocent III. However, since the pope accepted the challenge of the uncomfortable prophet, and recognized in Francis the man who was sustaining the collapsing walls of the Church, he, too, remained, in a decisive moment, a trustworthy teacher in the Church.

To all of us is granted the gracious word, *epheta* — open — but it is said first with reference to the ears and only then with reference to our lips. Our words can be wise and helpful only after we have listened. If all Christians were faithful to the charism of *epheta,* of sincere attention and ready and generous response, then the Church would never lack a magisterium of charismatic men and women: popes, bishops, theologians, pastors, teachers, parents.

It is above all a matter of integrated prayer, of listening to God, watching the signs of the times, discerning events in a mutual, shared reflection with other people of good will, in a united and co-operative effort to give the right response.

Those who listen intently to the word of God know that we cannot ignore the many modern instruments which help us to understand better the world around us. We cannot, for instance, ignore the behavioural sciences which tell us so much about man and his world. Whoever wants to proclaim the good news and give effective witness to it has to know the world into which we are sent. As Chesterton said, 'To teach John Latin, it is not enough to know Latin; you have also to know John.'

Prayer as well as life has to draw strength from the knowledge of God and the knowledge of man. This is possible only in constant openness to the word of both God and man. Only by

listening, then, can we live according to the basic programme
of the Second Vatican Council: 'The joys and the hopes, the
griefs and anxieties of the men of this age, especially those who
are poor or in any way afflicted, these too are the joys and
hopes, the griefs and anxieties of the followers of Christ' (The
Church in the modern world, 1).

✝ Dear Lord, I like the sweet music of the kind and gentle
words that come from my brothers and sisters. But I must also
open my ears and my heart to listen to what the life and the
cries of people have to tell me. Give me patience, O Lord, so
that I can listen to those whose words challenge and hurt me.
Give all of us the courage and the readiness to listen to the
uncomfortable prophets who call us to conversion, to healthy
but painful change. And let us listen, Lord, to our neighbour
when he calls us to greater generosity.

9. Christ, the Prophet

One of the names with which Christ is frequently honoured
in the gospel is 'The Prophet'.

Christ is not one among many prophets; he is The Prophet.
In him the history of ethical prophetism comes to its climax
and opens new vistas of history. The evangelists never call Christ
priest or high-priest; he is not a son of Aaron or of Levi; he
does not belong to a priestly class. The only salary he receives
from the priests is the death penalty, persecution and calumny.
Only the epistle to the Hebrews calls Christ the high-priest;
but it insists at the same time that his priesthood is wholly
different from that of Aaron: that Christ is the prophetic high-
priest and therefore no priesthood has value henceforth except
in and through the prophetic vocation of Christ. Christ does
not offer merely symbolic vows and ritual sacrifice; he offers
himself for the salvation of the whole world.

The great prophets of both the old and the new covenants

are distinguished by their capacity to integrate the sense of God and the sense of man. They experience the holiness and the mercy of God with such intensity that they become witnesses to his mercy on the poor, the discriminated against, and the sufferers.

The prophets cannot tolerate the gap between religion and life. They know that we cannot love God without loving our neighbour, and that the test comes with the neighbour who cannot repay us. For them, religion is the experience of God's gratuitous love, of the gift of his peace and justice to his people, who call for a reciprocity of justice, peace and love among themselves.

The prophets unite in one great synthesis the experience of God's holiness and the experience of his nearness. God is at the same time infinitely holy and also merciful beyond all human concepts. In the prayer of the prophets, the outcry of joy about God's nearness is united with the experience of their own sinfulness which, however, does not destroy them because they experience at the same time God's purifying mercy.

The whole history of Israel and a great part of the history of the Church manifest a sharp tension between a decaying clergy falling into all kinds of formalism, ritualism, lifeless legalism and careerism, and a prophetic renewal. However, we should not forget that in the Old Testament, some of the prophets who came from the priesthood families had already united in one great synthesis the adoration of God and the living of daily life, the vertical and the horizontal perspectives. And throughout the history of the Church many priests manifested a prophetic spirit.

Pope John is probably one of the most characteristic witnesses in our time to the ability to unite the best of the priestly and the prophetic traditions. Pope Paul follows in his footsteps by his pressing appeals for peace and justice, while at the same time he is concerned about a life of prayer and the priestly ministry of the word.

In Christ we have the perfect unity between adoration of the Father and infinite mercy on all men. Christ fulfils his prophetic mission on the cross, when he opens wide his arms and heart to all men for the glory of the one God and Father of all. He is the perfect adorer of God, adorer in spirit and in truth. Like all the prophets, Christ is on the side of the humble ones, the poor, the deprived, the widows and orphans. By his life and by his words he teaches us that the test of our love for God and our neighbour is our relationship to the poor who need our help and our respect, rather than to the rich and powerful who can reward us.

The lives of all the prophets are characterized by prophetic boldness and by the suffering that is often the price of it. The prophets do not enjoy their mission of criticizing the powerful, the kings, the priestly class, and sometimes the mass of the people; but as God sends them so does he also give them the necessary strength. However, there is no place in their life for sterile criticism. The frankness which shocks is always a part of the message of peace and of reconciliation, a promise of return to the Father for all those who accept the call to conversion.

Christ came to proclaim the gladdening news; but the obstinate minds of the priests and Pharisees compelled him to unmask their alienation in words that shock. Everything he says, however, is inspired by love for all men, even for those who are the objects of his prophetic frankness.

The prophets are not sent to save individual souls only. Their mission is characterized by a unique vision of wholeness. They urge the individual person to conversion and the whole people to renewal. Those who turn wholeheartedly to God will always commit themselves to the renewal of the Church and of the world around them. One cannot follow Christ the Prophet or pray in his name without seeking an existential synthesis between personal conversion and involvement in social, cultural, political, and ecclesiastical renewal.

The prophets open new horizons of transcendence and of

the absolute future, while discovering the grace of the present hour. Christ, the great Prophet, reveals to us the urgent appeal of the grace of God to profit by the hour that the Father has prepared for us, and to use the present opportunity in the perspective of the final kingdom of God in the world to come.

Nobody lives the present hour of decision so intensely as Christ; at the same time, his life and his paschal mystery promise us everlasting life. Not one single act of true love and justice will be lost in the kingdom of the Father. The promise of the communion of saints and of perfect beatitude with God allows no alienation; on the contrary, gratitude and hope, strengthened by the prophets, make possible a non-violent and patient commitment to the present moment, in view of a better future for all of mankind.

This perspective of Christ the Prophet is particularly important at this time in history when so many are worried only about the present moment. Either they live it in a distracted and superficial way, without coherence and continuity, or else they want to change the world at once. And since they have lost the dimension of transcendence and the hope of everlasting life, they become quickly violent if the world does not become as they want it here and now.

✝ We praise you, Father, all holy and all merciful God, because you have sent us Christ, the great Prophet.

We believe in the Holy Spirit who has spoken through the prophets, and especially through Christ, and who continues to speak through them in order to shake us, to awaken us, to encourage us. If we listen to them our faith in the Holy Spirit will be truthful. Help us to accept the uncomfortable prophets who ask from us greater sincerity and greater generosity.

Send us, O Lord, prophets: men and women distinguished by a profound knowledge of you and your Christ, who, by the sanctity of their lives and by their love for the poor and oppressed, will lead us to Christ the Prophet.

Grant to today's young, who long for authentic religious experience, educators who do not instruct them only with empty words but who also teach them by a life that can communicate the joy and strength of faith.

In the name of Christ the Prophet, we ask you to free us from the dichotomy that exists between religious forms and daily life, and to help us to overcome that polarization which separates people who, on one hand, are seeking only transcendental meditation, and on the other think they can change the world alone, without relying on your grace.

Free us, O Lord, from dissipation and superficiality which hinder us from following Christ the Prophet, and make us so vulnerable to all kinds of manipulation.

May all of our lives proclaim our faith in the Holy Spirit who gives life and makes possible truthful adoration of you, our Father, and love for all our brothers and sisters.

10. *Christ, our Hope*

The name 'Jesus', and all his other names, inspire hope and trust in God. Hope is faith in God, the loving God.

Christ is the promise to the patriarchs and prophets, a promise that for us is fulfilled beyond all expectations. 'Blessed are the eyes that see what you are seeing; because I tell you, many prophets and kings have longed to see what you are seeing and did not see it, and longed to hear what you are hearing and did not hear it' (Lk 10:23-24).

Yet for us, too, Christ is still a promise, because we are still on our way and the world is still longing for the final liberation. But Christ is with us on our way. He comes constantly into our life as the promise 'already' realized and the firm but 'not-yet' totally fulfilled hope. As we discover his presence in our life more and more vitally, we long more and more to stay near him, to be with him.

But we cannot remain with him if we expect simply to sit and wait for the *parousia,* or if we look for a Church that gives assurance to those who do not want to be on the move. Christ is the hope of the pilgrim Church and of all those who accept the grace and the necessity of a continuous conversion and renewal. His promises and his presence keep us free from any kind of alienation from life, and give us strength and endurance on our way to the heavenly Jerusalem.

We are truly on the way with Christ, our Hope and our Promise, if we live a life of thanksgiving for all that God has already revealed and done, and of vigilance for what he wants us to do in the present moment, even if he wants to surprise us and lead us where we did not want to go. For those who put their trust in Christ, everything, even the most insignificant or the most unpleasant event, becomes a sign of grace and hope, a school of vigilance for the coming of our Lord.

Christ gives us hope because he has not come to seek his own pleasure or his own will but only the loving will of the Father. Having taken upon himself the burden of sinful mankind, he is 'the man for all people', the incarnate solidarity. We do not call him 'my Hope'; we call him 'our Hope', since he is for all, and all are called in one hope. Therefore, when we live with Christ our Hope, we cannot have a self-centred outlook on life. We praise his name by supporting each other, encouraging each other in difficult moments, and helping to bear the burdens of our discouraged neighbour.

Christ is our Hope also because he is the Faithful one. Beyond all our sins and failures, he remains faithful to his saving design.

I have met a family that could be called a sacrament of Christ our Hope. The wife, a good but sentimentally weak person, went through a terrible crisis and had sexual intercourse with a friend. With an anguished heart, she finally confessed to her husband that she was pregnant by someone else. Her husband said nothing. He embraced her, and then turned to the Lord and said, 'Lord, you have so often accepted us after our sins, that now I accept my wife with even greater love. Her child will be my child, since it is only through your mercy that we are all your sons and daughters.' The boy who was born to his wife was accepted as his son, and never came to know that he was not a flesh-and-blood son, since he always received the same love, the same acceptance as his brothers and sisters.

✢ O Christ, you are our hope. Without you we can do nothing that would have value for the salvation of mankind. All hope and all grace come from your death and resurrection.

Teach us, O Lord, to pray truthfully in your name. Free us from our foolish trust in ourselves and in the works of our hands and minds. Help us to pray in absolute trust that whatever you send us is for our good; and help us to accept the surprising things for which we have not prayed. Give us the trust that all events, even suffering and death, are for us occasions to glorify you and, with you, the Father.

And since you are the hope and salvation for all, we beg you, Lord, to free us from all kinds of selfishness and from individualism in matters of religion. Help us all to seek together peace and justice, respect and encouragement for everyone.

11. Christ, the Divine Physician

The ancient Church, which was much more conscious than we are of her healing ministry, liked to invoke Christ under the name 'Healer' or 'Divine Healer'.

Wherever Christ came, people brought the sick to him and he healed them. For him, healing was so urgent that the legalism of the Pharisees, who wanted him to stop healing on the Sabbath, provoked his holy wrath. Everyone wanted to touch him, come close to him, because a healing power 'went out from him'. This healing power is his love and his trust in the power of the Father.

To whatever degree our Church has trust in God, to that degree she exercises the healing ministry so explicitly entrusted to her by Christ. And to that same degree she becomes a community which encourages her members through mutual love and trust, and teaches them that to render thanks to the Father always and everywhere is a healing event.

Christ did not come to judge the world but to save it and to heal it. When he is confronted with sick people whose ailments have some relation to sin, he does not judge or condemn them but heals them by forgiving their sins and granting them the messianic peace. Even when he speaks as a prophet and unmasks self-deception and lies, the diagnosis which shocks aims solely at healing and salvation.

We cannot know existentially the name of Jesus Christ, the Divine Healer, or pray to him, unless we thoroughly renounce our attitude of judging others, despising and condemning them, and interpreting their intentions viciously. Whenever we meet others with absolute respect, with love, whenever we give credit and awaken in our fellowmen a trust in God and a healthy trust in themselves and in the community, we are abiding in Christ the Healer, and he is abiding in us. Then we can pray in his name; and indeed we must unceasingly pray in the name of Christ the Healer, because the pharisaical tendency to judge others, and even to write them off, is deeply rooted in our sinful nature.

We pray and act in the name of Christ, the Divine Physician, when our energies and our imagination unite in an effort to reform the vindictive system of human justice. We need to think more about changing institutions and the social environment, and about re-educating those who offend the law, than about locking them in the poisoned atmosphere of the present prison system where they are numbers, non-persons, outcasts. It is not only individuals but a sick society that is in need of healing.

It belongs to the ethos of the physician that he is a 'man for the other'. He is always ready to receive anyone who has urgent need of his healing powers. To know Jesus Christ, the Divine Physician, makes us available for others, and that availability and love for others makes us imaginative about how to deal with their wounds. How much greater would be the healing capacity of the medical profession if all of us together, and doctors in a particular way, were Christlike, if we showed such healing love and respect as Christ showed, and could awaken in people such great trust and faith as he awakened!

Fraternal correction, if it is offered with gentleness and with that humility which never forgets our own weaknesses and our own need of brotherly or sisterly help, can greatly contribute to that divine *milieu* in which we can call upon Christ, the Divine Physician.

✛ O Divine Physician, salvation of the sick and refuge of sinners, we come to you with an acute awareness of our need to be healed by you. Free us from our blindness, our selfishness and our tendencies to judge others who need rather to experience our healing understanding and generous help.

Dear Lord, we are living in a world that seems like a great hospital in which we find an enormous number of administrators and judges but only a few true doctors and nurses who are generous helpers able to heal, to understand, to encourage.

Lord, give to your Church priests, confessors, who conscientiously deny themselves the arrogant satisfaction of judging others and who, freed from ritualistic scrupulosity, can lead us, as your mirror-image, to you, the Divine Physician.

O Divine Physician, send forth your Spirit, that your Church may become ever more a divine *milieu* that heals, trusts and unites people to praise you and to manifest to each other your healing love.

Grant us men and women who are able to encourage each other and to offer fraternal correction with that humanness and kindness that leads to you.

12. *Jesus, the Good Shepherd*

Already in the Old Testament, God manifests his name as 'Shepherd of Israel'. Those in power too often exploit the people; the kings tend to be domineering. Therefore the scripture seldom uses the word 'king' to express God's sovereignty and exercise of authority; it is far better expressed in the image of the shepherd who loves his flock.

When King David had become unfaithful to his mission as shepherd of Israel, the prophet Nathan reproved him with a parable about a good shepherd's kindness: 'The poor man had nothing at all but one little lamb that he had bought. He nourished her, and she grew up with him and his children; she shared the little food he had, and drank from his cup and slept in his bosom' (2 Sam 12:3).

The prophet Ezekiel exhorts the rulers of Israel to become worthy of the title, 'Shepherd of Israel'. 'Woe to the shepherds of Israel who have been pasturing themselves... For thus says the Lord: I myself will look after and tend my sheep. As a shepherd tends his flock when he finds himself among his scattered sheep, so will I tend my sheep. I will rescue them from every place where they were scattered when it was cloudy and dark. I will lead them back to their own country and pasture, and pasture them upon the mountains of Israel... I myself will pasture my sheep; I myself will give them rest. The lost I will seek out; the strayed I will bring back; the injured I will bind up; the sick I will heal, shepherding them rightly' (Ezek 34:2-16).

The messianic king is announced as the good shepherd: 'I will appoint one shepherd over them to pasture them, my servant; he shall pasture them and be their shepherd ... thus they shall know that I, the Lord, am their God and that they are my people, the house of Israel, says the Lord God' (Ezek 34:23-30).

The shepherds of Bethlehem are among the first to make known the coming of the Saviour. Between the shepherds and the angels, there is a wonderful affinity as messengers of peace to all men of good will.

Christ repeatedly calls himself the good shepherd promised by the prophets. 'I am the good shepherd; the good shepherd lays down his life for the sheep... I am the good shepherd; I know my sheep and they know me, as the Father knows me and I know the Father; for these sheep I will give my life' (Jn 10: 13-16).

These moving words tell us what the Bible means by 'to know'. In the same loving and intimate way that he knows the Father, the source of all love, Christ knows us. He knows his friends better than the good shepherd knows the sheep in his flock. And we can know him, his life, his love and his salvation, to the extent that we listen to his voice calling us to follow him, and more, to love the others in his flock as he loves us.

Christ is the good shepherd who, with infinite love, seeks the lost sheep, not to punish it but to take it on his shoulders and bring it home. He, the shepherd, wants so much to bring all the lost sheep of Israel and of all nations home to the Father, that he is ready to lay down his life for them.

Of course not all lost sheep are ready to return the moment they are found; but when they finally do return, their own joy is a ray of the joy in heaven. I remember such a case when, in 1947, I used my vacation time to preach a kind of parish retreat for Catholic refugees, displaced persons and others living in Protestant areas where there was not yet any organized pastoral care for them.

One of the refugees, an old school teacher, helped me to round up the Catholics. He was a man of strong moral principles and, as he said, a 'man of honour'. Often he hesitated to tell me that this or that family was Catholic because, he told me, he felt ashamed to call them Catholics. At the very end, he pointed to a house and said, 'Well, you want to know them all. In that house is also a Catholic, a prostitute for American soldiers. I hope you will be a man of honour and not visit her'. However I insisted, and told him that although he was a man of honour, he should accompany me. But we came at the wrong moment. She was with another girl of the same dubious profession, and therefore we were received with great hostility. My friend said, 'Didn't I tell you?'

However, the next day, ignoring the names she had called us, I went again to her house and invited her once more to come to hear the word of God, which could also be a comforting word for her. She responded reluctantly, 'Well, since you have been so courteous, I must accept your invitation; but I shall come only once, no more'. So she came that evening — and the next evening, and all the following ones; and the following week she and her older children came even to the next little town, four miles away. She made her peace with the Lord. And when I returned the following year, my old friend told me, 'The lady whom I called such bad names, and who therefore had a right to call me bad names too, is a totally new person. Her five children are also completely different from what they were before'.

This poor lady had begun to sell her body at a time of greatest need, when she had no food for her children, and could get no food except by selling herself. Do we not too often write people off instead of making Christ the Good Shepherd known to them?

The word 'pastor', by which we honour priests, bishops and the pope, means the same as 'shepherd': it means that they should know the members of their flocks, care for them, lead them to the high, green pastures of the knowledge and love of God, seek out the lost ones and bring them home and thus, by their whole being and ministry, make known to them Christ the Good Shepherd.

But they are not the only ones who should be shepherds. All members of the Church, and in a special way married couples, parents, teachers, guardians, should, by their loving responsibility for the members of their families and for those entrusted to them by their office or by particular circumstances, lead them to an ever better knowledge of Jesus the Good Shepherd, and to the consciousness of his presence with them.

If we pray and act in the name of Jesus the Good Shepherd, then we are already coming to a deeper understanding of all our brothers and sisters, and to more compassion and generosity towards them, and especially towards those who are like lost sheep, those with whom nobody falls in love, and who first need great love, encouragement and respect before we can expect from them a satisfying response.

✢   O Divine Shepherd, forgive me for so often failing to care about my brothers and my neighbour. I was not their friend or their healer because I did not know you, the Good Shepherd. I did not do everything in my power, did not pray and meditate to know you better so that I could make you known to those around me. And how could I know you, when I did not learn, either, to deepen my understanding of my brothers and sisters and their real needs, their thoughts, and their rightful desires?

So many of your people have gone astray, Divine Shepherd! What offence it must be to you when those who are called to be the shepherds of nations, of your people, the guardians of the rights of the innocent, assert that mothers and doctors have the right to kill, whenever they please, the innocent life in the mother's womb? Yet how can these mothers know you, the Good Shepherd? They are like lost sheep, confused by a poisoned public opinion, manipulated by a society of consumers and individualists who call this most inhuman and atrocious action a 'human right', a 'right to privacy'. Their thinking has been debauched by hidden persuaders and overt manipulators. Nor are those without guilt who, while rightly proclaiming the abstract right to live, have made no realistic effort to create the conditions of life that make the child welcome to the mother and to this world that you have given for all. Indeed, do we not all share in the guilt? Help us, O Lord, to be good shepherds for them and to find effective means to protect mothers and physicians from this abominable temptation.

Manifest yourself, O Lord, to your people as the Good Shepherd. Grant us time and grace for repentance and conversion. Grant that the pastors of your Church may be authentic images of you, free from greed and from the desire to have the first place and the highest title. Let their only endeavour be to lead your people to an ever greater knowledge of you and of the needs of their fellowmen. Lead us all to unity and brotherhood, since this is the good pasture you have promised to your people.

Awaken, O Lord, in all those who occupy important offices, the spirit of responsibility, that they may do everything possible to know the real needs and the dignity of those who are entrusted to them. Make them a sign of your presence in the world, as men and women who do not look so much to be served as to serve.

13. *Christ, the Liberator and Redeemer*

We live in a world of built-in slavery. Sin is slavery and alienation. It surrounds and holds us in a web of incarnate egotism of individuals, groups and institutions.

What the Bible calls 'the sin of the world' is, more than anything else, greed and the desire to dominate and to exploit others. A person in today's world is manipulated in a thousand ways and, without realizing it, manipulates others. Modern means of communication, which are wonderful gifts of God, become tools of exploitation in the hands of economic powers and pressure groups. Modern psychology, too, is exploited to find new ways to arouse feelings and desires that make people vulnerable to the influence of the idols of power, the idols of the market.

On the other hand, today's generation knows — or should know — that people can gradually free themselves from unfavourable conditions and manipulations if they use all the knowledge that is now accessible to them, and work together for freedom in imaginative, non-violent and creative endeavour. Mankind is longing for liberation.

In scripture, Christ is called Redeemer and Liberator; and indeed these two words are most intimately related. Yahweh manifests himself as the redeemer, the saviour, when he frees his people from the slavery of Egypt. When, therefore, we call upon Christ the Redeemer, we join our efforts with his intention to free mankind from the slavery of sin and the sin of slavery. We pray in his name for the great gift of the liberty of the sons and daughters of God.

Christ is the redeemer not only of souls and of separate individuals; he is the redeemer of the whole person and of the whole world. He wants to restore man's wholeness and liberty. 'Thus says the Lord: In a time of favour I have heard you; in the days of liberation I helped you to restore the land and all the desolated heritages: saying to the prisoners "Come out", and to those in darkness, "Show yourselves" ' (Is 49: 8-9).

Christ has come as Liberator. 'The Spirit of the Lord is upon me; therefore he has anointed me; he has sent me to bring glad tidings to the poor, to proclaim liberty to the captives and recovery of sight to the blind, and release to the oppressed; to announce the favourable year of the Lord' (Lk 4: 18-19).

We can pray and act in the name of Christ the Redeemer when we are truly freeing ourselves and are working not only for an individualized freedom but for freedom for all, especially those most oppressed, most discriminated against and outcast.

To pray in the name of Christ the Liberator is to ask him for endurance and generosity in our commitment to peace and to a freer, more brotherly and more just world. We pray for insight, for imagination and the spirit of initiative, for personal responsibility and a sense of co-responsibility that brings us all together in the great mission of liberation for all. We pray, too, for the vigilance and the courage to grasp every opportunity to foster the spirit of liberty and liberation in institutions, in public opinion, in our environment, and in the understanding and application of law and of moral principles.

The more we commit ourselves to the building up of a divine *milieu* in which prevails the spirit of goodness, gentleness, non-violence, sincerity, justice, and respect for the freedom of all, the more we come to a deeper knowledge of Christ and also of the appropriate means to advance the cause of freedom in the world around us. Thus we proclaim the name of Jesus, the Liberator and Redeemer.

✠ O Christ, Redeemer, illumine us so that we may see all the wonderful effort your friends have made and are making for freedom, and yet see also our own misery, our being manipulated and conditioned by so many subtle pressures which have their source in individual sins and in our collective pride, arrogance and greed. Awaken us to the extent of our share in collective prejudices, in manipulation, in depreciation of other cultures and of people of other social classes.

By the power of your Spirit, let us discern what true freedom is, and accept the limited opportunities of that freedom which will grow in our minds, our hearts and our wills if we commit ourselves to you, the one Redeemer, in the cause of freedom for all persons.

I know, O Lord, that I cannot pray in your name as Redeemer and Liberator if I do not want to become free, to grow out of my narrowness and my individualistic outlook. Around us, so many people and ideologies are crying, 'Liberty, liberty', without knowing what that freedom is for which you came to liberate us.

Let your Holy Spirit come upon us, that we may learn to discern and to feel the longing of all creation to have a share in the freedom of your sons and daughters. Make us generous enough to renounce even legitimate expressions of our own freedom wherever they are not conducive to the common freedom. Thus we can trust that you will open up new insights and possibilities for the better expression of our freedom, and send us to make known to all the world that you are the only true liberator.

14. *Christ, the Reconciliation*

Christ the Prophet unmasks self-deception and deception of others, especially by those pious liars who talk of peace where there is no peace but only manipulation and the competition of power structures. He does not make his peace with arrogant manipulators who use power, chicanery or violence to retain an unjust *status quo* or to gain even greater and more vicious control over their fellowmen.

Christ came to expose and to destroy false peace and promises of peace in order to bring true peace. His whole life and his word is a two-edged sword that lays bare the hidden thoughts and intentions of the unjust. Yet he who is announced by the prophet as 'Wonderful Counsellor and Prince of Peace' (Is 9:5) comes from the Father with the angels' song, 'Peace on earth to all men of good will'. His whole intention is peace, even when he drives the sacred liars from the temple and confronts the Pharisees and the unworthy high priests with challenging protest. Even when the evil he is denouncing provokes anger in him, his words arise from a deep peace and are an appeal for peace. In all events and to all people, he offers himself as peacemaker and reconciler.

Christ, the Word Incarnate, takes upon himself the conflict and suffering of the sinful world. He is both the saving conflict and the reconciliation. He bears peace for us — peace with the Father and peace among us — even in the midst of the terrible storms of his passion and crucifixion.

We ourselves have done nothing to deserve the peace that Christ offers us; it is an absolutely gratuitous gift of the Father. Only when we are fully and humbly aware of this gratuitousness can we receive and preserve his peace, in thankfulness for the One who has suffered and died for us sinners so that we may be reconciled with the Father and with each other. Only those who pray with unceasing gratitude to him who is the source of all peace can rejoice in the fullness of his peace. And the truthfulness of our gratitude can be expressed only by committing ourselves to be peacemakers always, whatever the cost.

Christ bears peace and reconciliation for all people. It is impossible, therefore, to accept his peace and to abide in it if we do not allow him to transform us into channels of peace and ambassadors of reconciliation. Whoever truly knows Christ as our Peace and Reconciliation will ever pray with Francis, 'Lord, make me an instrument of your peace'.

If we want to pray and act in the name of Christ our Reconciler, then we have to face the situations of conflict in our own lives. We are living in a divided society and a factious Church where there is often painful stress. This constitutes for us an urgent appeal to turn our thoughts decisively to the name of Christ the Reconciler. The main cause of the manifold quarrels and divisions in our society and ecclesial communities is always the egotism and pride of the individuals and groups involved. Yet Christ came and died for us to free us from these evils of division: 'The love of Christ impels us who have reached the conviction that since one died for all, all died. He died for all so that those who live might no longer live selfishly for themselves but for him who for their sakes died and was raised up. This means that anyone who is in Christ is a new creation. The old order has passed away; now all is new. All this has been done by God who has reconciled us to himself through Christ and has given us the ministry of reconciliation. I mean that God, in Christ, was reconciling the world to himself, not counting men's transgressions against them, and thus he has entrusted the message of reconciliation to us. This makes us ambassadors for Christ, God, as it were, appealing through us. We implore you in Christ's name, be reconciled to God' (2 Cor 5: 14-20).

The very special ministry of reconciliation is entrusted to the successors of Peter, to bishops and to priests. To an exceptional degree, therefore, they need the knowledge of Christ, our

Peace and Reconciliation. But if we believe in the universal priesthood of the faithful, then all of us will constantly pray in the name of Christ, not only for our own reconciliation with the Father, but also that by our own actions and attitudes we may become ever more able to make Christ known as Peace.

Christ has clearly shown us that the two dimensions of peace — peace with the Father and peace among ourselves — cannot be separated. It is also clear that the gratuitous character of Christ's reconciliation and peace is the strongest motive for us to be co-workers with him and co-revealers of his peace to all people.

✛ O Christ, Reconciliation for all mankind, free us from our selfishness, from our narrowness, and from the pride that bears the bitter fruit of 'hostilities, jealousy, outbursts of rage, selfish rivalries, dissensions, factions, envy' (Gal 5: 21). Let your Spirit come upon us all, that we may reap the harvest of the Spirit: 'love, joy, peace, patience, endurance, kindness, generosity, faith, gentleness, and self-control' (Gal 5: 22).

Give us the courage and the strength to put to death our own selfishness and to fight a valiant battle against all the conditionings and structures that destroy your peace and hinder reconciliation among men and nations.

You, O Lord, have paid the highest price for our reconciliation and that of the world. Give us the generosity to go the way of the cross with you, so that we may radiate your peace to all around us.

15. *Christ, Son of God and Son of Man*

In our profession of faith we proclaim the names of Jesus, 'only Son of the Father, eternally begotten of the Father, God from God, Light from Light, true God from true God'. We also confess his name as 'the son of man, born of the Virgin

Mary', who thus made himself our brother, the man for all mankind.

Christ is alone the perfect monotheist. He is revealed as true Son, upon whom the favour of the Father rests, by his embracing all the sons and daughters of the Father and bearing the burdens of his brothers and sisters for all time. This universal brotherhood is the thanks he renders to the Father for having united his humanity with his Eternal Word.

The very heart of our faith, of our prayer, and of our whole life is to know and to recognize Christ as true God and true man, the only begotten Son of the Father and the son of man. We must be warned against past tendencies which either so exalted the Godhead of Christ that his humanity was forgotten, or else emphasized so much his true humanity that his divine dignity was forgotten or even denied. Only if we love Christ as God and as man, as our Lord and as our brother, can we be truthful and faithful to him who came to unite, in one unique synthesis, the love of God and love for all men.

Christ makes known to us the name of God, 'Father', by his own trust and his praise of the Father, Lord of heaven and earth, to whom he entrusts himself with his last breath on the cross: 'Father, into your hands I entrust my spirit'. He manifests the name of God as, at the same time, his Father and our Father, by making himself the Man for all the Father's children, thus tearing down the barriers that separate human races and groups.

There is only one way to honour Christ authentically as true God and true man, as the Son of the Father and the son of man, and that is by commiting ourselves thoroughly to the fulfilment of his last prayer, 'That all may be one, as you, Father, and I are one; you in me and I in you. I pray that they may be one in us, that the world may believe that you sent me' (Jn 17: 21).

✝ We praise you, Lord, who from all eternity are the Son of

the Father. You have shown us the Father by becoming one like us in all things except sin. You lead us to the one Father by opening your heart and your arms to all his sons and daughters, who are your brothers and sisters, and ours.

As the Son of the Father and the son of man, teach us how to adore and to honour our Father. Send us your Holy Spirit, that all our lives may cry out joyously, 'Abba, Father! Our Father!' For we honour and glorify his name as Father if we, like you, love and respect our brethren.

16. *Christ, Emmanuel* — *'God with us'*

The name 'Emmanuel' is already announced by the prophet: 'The Lord himself will give you this sign. The virgin shall be with child, and her son they shall name Emmanuel' (Is 7: 14).

This name of Jesus spells out the same truth as the name 'True God and true man': God is with us. In a very special way it invites us to pray to him, to open ourselves to an ever-growing awareness of his nearness and his friendship, and to centre our attention on him who, always and forever, comes into our life. The name 'God-with-us' can be known existentially — can be really experienced — only by those who are attuned to him, who take the time to listen to him, who rejoice in him and praise him for his friendship.

The whole Bible, but especially the New Testament, the life of the Church, her liturgy and her saints, make known to us the name Emmanuel. Those who had the privilege of living with Jesus, as Mary and Joseph did in the house of Nazareth, knew with infinite joy what this name means. The disciples experienced it. The invitation 'Follow me' was not just a word spoken by anyone; it was a word coming from the fascinating person, Jesus. He is the Emmanuel.

In the sermon on the mount, which is a synthesis of the whole gospel and the law of the gospel, we see Jesus 'in the presence of the crowd' (Mt 5:1) with his disciples 'gathered close around him'. It is from his gracious presence that the beatitudes radiate. He himself is gentleness, compassion and peace incarnate, he who is called the Son of God and the brother of all. The deep meaning of the words of the sermon on the mount can be understood only by those who know the meaning of the name Emmanuel, the loving presence of Jesus Christ, not only to the few disciples but to the crowd.

When Moses received the law of the covenant on Mount Sinai, he was alone with God. Because of their stubbornness, Aaron and the people — the crowd — could not even approach the mountain on which God revealed himself. But since the Eternal Word came to us in our humanity and decided to dwell 'with us', the conversion which allows us to experience his nearness, his friendship, became possible and urgent for us. And being close to him, we are friends with each other. Jesus, Emmanuel, brought us close to himself and to each other.

This is also the chief message of the farewell discourses. Before the disciples, Christ stands, the perfect sacrament, the fully visible image of the love of the heavenly Father. And he who is the Lord meets his disciples as the most humble servant; the one who is so near to his friends is the Lord. 'You call me Master and Lord, and fittingly enough; for that is what I am' (Jn 13:13).

But his nearness does not allow the disciples to forget that he is truly the Lord, the Redeemer and Liberator of all the world. Therefore, only those can rejoice in his name, Emmanuel, who by their life honour his name as Lord. 'Not all of those who cry out Lord, Lord, will enter the kingdom of God, but only those who do the will of my Father in heaven... Anyone who hears my words and puts them into practice is like the wise man who built his house on a rock' (Mt 7:21-24).

Again and again Christ tells his disciples how vital it is to know him as Emmanuel. 'Live in me as I do in you. No more than the branch can bear fruit apart from the vine, can you bear fruit apart from me. I am the vine, you are the branches. He who lives in me and I in him will bear fruit abundantly' (Jn 15:4-5).

Our response to this name is the heart and dynamic of prayer and of its value and capacity to transform us. 'If you live in me and my words become a part of you, you may ask what you will and it will be done for you' (Jn 15:7). Whoever lives in gratitude for the name Emmanuel will experience the joy of the Lord. 'All this I tell you, that my joy may be yours and that your joy may be complete' (Jn 15:11).

It is because of the presence of God himself in our hearts, through the power of the Holy Spirit, that we can honour the name Emmanuel as the Lord of all mankind, Lord of the world. 'If you love me and keep the commands I give you, I will ask the Father and he will send you another Paraclete to abide with you always, the Spirit of truth... You can recognize him because he remains with you and will be within you' (Jn 14:15-17).

When we truly know the name Emmanuel, and unite it with the name Lord, then we also know that the commandments of God are not something coming from afar. Whoever abides in the Lord is aware that he teaches us his law by his nearness, by his presence. 'The graciousness of God has appeared, offering salvation to all people. It teaches us to reject godless ways and selfish desires, and to live temperately, justly and devoutly in this age, as we await our blessed hope, the appearance of the glory of our great God and Saviour, Jesus Christ' (Titus 2:11-13).

Our joy in the nearness of the Lord in our prayer, and in a life with him and for him, is only a beginning that makes us long for an ever deeper experience of his graciousness. We look forward to the blessed coming of him who, for all eternity, will be our Saviour and Emmanuel, God-with-us. To be with him forever is our hope, and we experience the power of hope whenever we pray in the name of Jesus, the Emmanuel. 'This is God's dwelling among them. He shall dwell with them and they shall be his people and he shall be their God who is always with them' (Rev 21:3).

Our response to the revelation of the name Emmanuel can be only joy, trust and praise. 'God indeed is my saviour. I am confident and unafraid. My strength and my courage is the Lord and he has been my saviour. In joy you will draw water at the fountain of salvation and say on that day: "Give thanks to the Lord, acclaim his name; among the nations make known his deeds and proclaim how exalted is his name. Shout with exultation, O city of Sion, for great in your midst is the holy one of Israel" ' (Is 12:2-6).

✤ O Emmanuel, come to your people. Open our eyes and purify our hearts by the power of your Spirit. Convert us to you, that we may come to a more profound understanding of your name Emmanuel, and have life and joy in you.

What a great honour it is to be called your disciples and your friends, and to be sent as messengers of your peace and co-workers for your reconciliation!

We can live up to this honour and fulfil your mission only if we entrust ourselves to you, abide with you, treasure up your message in us, and thus experience the joy of your name, Emmanuel.

Come, O come, Emmanuel, and abide with your people.

17. *The names of God*

To know the names of our Saviour is to know and to praise the name of the Father whom he reveals to us. All the previous meditations and prayers lead us to the One whose Name is beyond all names.

✤ With Moses we ask, 'What is your Name? How shall we call you, who have given the name to all men and all things?'

And through your beloved Son, Jesus Christ, you have answered:

I am the *Father*. You are my child. Honour all my children, revere all people — and you will know me.

I am the almighty *Creator*. Your life and all that you have is my gift to you. Adore me with all of your being, always and everywhere — and you will know me.

I am *Love* and the power of love. Ask me for the supreme power, the power to love me and, with me, to love my people — and you will know me.

I am *Fidelity*. Trust in my promises and keep your promises — and you will know me.

I am infinite *Mercy*. Be merciful to the poor, the weak, the sinner — and you will know me.

I am all *Goodness*. Rely on my goodness and show goodness to others — and you will know me.

I am *Purity of heart*. Love your neighbour with a pure heart, with no thought of reward — and you will know me.

I am *Benevolence*. Respect my whole creation and be benevolent to all your brethren — and you will know me.

I am your *Providence*. Care for the present moment and look forward to the future with responsibility but also with trust — and you will know me.

I am *Gentleness*. Blessed are those of a gentle spirit. They make known my name to many. Be one of them — and you will know me.

I am *Beauty*. Open your eyes to all my works. Contemplate them — and you will know me.

I am *Joy* and *Beatitude*. Rejoice in me and bring joy to all whom you meet — and you will know me.

I am *Justice*. Be just and serve justice through non-violent action. Help those who suffer from the injustice of sinful man — and you will know me.

I am *Peace*. Find your rest in me and be grateful for my

peace. Accept your mission to be a channel of peace — and you will know me.

I am *Reconciliation*. In the midst of all tensions, I am the reconciling and healing love. Be my ambassador of reconciliation; seek unity and accord in justice — and you will know me.

I am *Grace*. Be gracious to all persons. Appreciate their graciousness and generosity — and you will know me.

I am *Life*. Be grateful for every moment of your life. Protect the life of all human beings. Use to the full the present moment — and you will know me.

I am *Truth*. Be truthful with yourself and sincere with all others. Live your own life and prepare to die your own death. Act according to your upright conscience, seeking always for more light — and you will know me.

I am *The Judge*. Confess your sins; forgive those who have wronged you. Honour my saving judgement, remembering that I alone am judge — and you will know me.

I am *The Holy One,* who calls you to holiness. Trust in me, believe in me, adore me in spirit and truthfulness — and you will know me.

I am *The Beginning and the End*. Begin everything in my name, and direct all your steps to me — and, in life and in death, you will know me.

✝ I praise you, Father, Lord of heaven and earth, because you have revealed your name through your Son, Jesus Christ.

You have sought me, calling me by name. Now I call upon your name, for I have begun to know you, and want to know you more and more. I shall knock on your door each day, knowing that you will open for me the door to eternal life, where I shall know your perfection and be with you for evermore.

Chapter 2

THE PRESENCE OF GOD
AS THE BASIS OF PRAYER

Prayer is a conscious and responsive life in the presence of God. We can pray and experience prayer as the most vital expression of our being because God is present; he comes into our life; he is with us.

Through a Christian life, the growth of faith manifests itself in every particular way, in the discovery of ever new dimensions and joys of God's presence. His being with us gives us life, consciousness, the ability to listen and respond, and to express ourselves as his friends by our words and deeds.

What does 'presence' mean? It means an empathetic 'being with'. One does not speak of the 'presence' of an inanimate object; it is simply there. Only persons can be present to each other; and there is authentic presence only when persons turn their attention and love to each other. If I am in a crowd waiting for a train or bus, where nobody cares for the other, I cannot speak of 'presence' but only of the lonely crowd. If someone calls upon me, meets me, wants to be loved and understood by me, and I refuse, I fail to realize presence. Refusing the other's desire for presence, I am alienated.

Presence can have different degrees of intensity. Two

persons who meet to discuss business or to carry out a common task without being interested in each other will be far from realizing the kind of presence experienced by those who meet to express their friendship, their affection and fidelity.

To live fully in the presence of others, one has to realize one's own presence and has to locate it in the present moment. The old grandfather, talking endlessly about 'the good old times' is not truly present to us; he has already partially faded away. Only those who see the 'now' in its true dimensions, aware of the past and open to the future, perceive the grace of the present moment and are able to meet others in a real mutuality of presence.

The prototype of presence is the union of husband and wife, their loving attention to each other, their being totally for each other. The mother remains present to her little child even when she sleeps. As soon as the child needs her, she will be awake and totally available to the child.

There is no way to the eternal God for those who do not appreciate the present moment, and there is no chance to experience the living presence of God for those who do not appreciate the presence of their friends, their neighbours, and are not present to them through affection and respect.

The presence of persons created in the image and likeness of God is a kind of sacrament, a real symbol of God's own loving presence. But as soon as we come to a deeper experience of God himself, and believe with all our hearts in his creative and redemptive presence in our life, we shall also be far more able to be present to others and to discover the wealth of the present moment.

✝ I thank you, Father, for all the loving persons who have come into my life, and for all those who have accepted my own effort to respect them and to lend them a helping hand. All that I am now is to a great extent the gift of those who were, at any moment of my life, present to me and allowed me to be present to them.

Grant us, O Lord, the wisdom to live fully the present moment and our presence to each other, as we travel the road to an abiding presence with you.

1. *The presence of God in his creation*

In our reflections about important spiritual truths, it is always good to start with the first article of our faith: I believe in one God, the Creator and Father Almighty.

The event of creation, as presented in scripture, becomes the foundation of our faith and an abiding invitation to a life that unfolds in the conscious presence of God, the Creator.

The proof of God's existence offered in the categories of Aristotle, with arguments of causality — prime causality and secondary causality — may have value as an intellectual exercise, but it is a religious or non-religious talk. Quite different is the word of the Bible about God's manifestation of his presence through all of his works.

Creation is a word, an event, in which God manifests his will as a loving design of Presence. The Spirit who renews the face of the earth is symbolized by the mighty wind that swept over the surface of the waters when God said, 'Let there be light, and there was light' (Gen 1: 2-3). All the created universe is a glorious word of God who reveals himself as Light and Truth.

God does not make a show just for himself; his every word is to communicate himself to humankind. And the whole history of evolution reaches out dynamically to the moment when man understands God's word and can admire and respond. 'And God said, "Let us make man in our image, after our likeness" ' (Gen 1: 26).

God calls all of us to be his co-workers and co-creators in his world. As soon as he has created us, he invites us to find our repose, our joy with him. That is what is meant by the Sabbath: man earns his dignity by taking part in the ongoing creation. However, only when we can rejoice in the presence of the One who has called us to work and to walk with him and to be finally with him, do we prove our authenticity and identity as we submit the earth to ourselves to make it a human environment.

That the whole of creation is a word that invites mankind to presence, to praise, to thanksgiving, is made explicit in the New Testament. 'When all things began, the Word already was. The Word was with God, and what God was, the Word was. The Word was with God in the beginning, and with him all things came to be. No single thing is created without him; all that came to be is alive with his life' (Jn 1: 1-4).

It is a poor kind of man who looks around him only to use things. We truly reach the stature of a person only when we can admire, can listen to the sound of the wind, to the song of all creation, and especially to the words of our fellowmen. Everything is a gratuitous gift of God who creates us as sharers of his love; hence everything invites us to trust, to gratitude, to a response.

And since, in all these realities, God manifests himself, his own life, his own love, everything is an appeal to us to respond with all our being, by bringing everything home to our Creator. Creation itself appeals to us to order the world around us in a way that explicitly honours God, the Creator, and all men created in his image and likeness.

Man is not a robot, not a cog in a wheel. He finds his true name when he takes time to celebrate the Sabbath, time for reflection, for awakening himself to the fullest possible awareness of God's presence. This is the necessary condition for a life of activity and responsibility in which everything is a response to God.

Those who do not find the proper synthesis between prayer and work, reflection and action, become slaves of their own tools. If they do not admire God's work, do not praise him and thank him, they forfeit the paradise, deprive themselves of the consciousness of God's presence, and thus become restless.

✝   May all my life express my faith in you, Father Almighty, Creator of heaven and earth. You are present and speak to me in the beauty of the firmament, in the wonders of the animal world, in birdsong and floral splendour, and above all, in the countenances of your people whom you have created in the image of your goodness.

As Father, you have created everything in your almighty Word, in whom you express your own wisdom and love. Everything is a gift to your children, a message that proclaims to us your love, the same love that, from all eternity, you express in your Word, your only begotten Son.

You have, created everything, visible and invisible, and thus have manifested not only your majesty and power but, even more, your loving care for all your children.

Grant that in your gifts I may see your own presence with such intensity that they will become gifts in my hands too. Let them be signs of love for my brothers and sisters, and of solidarity with them, to honour you, the only Father and Creator, and your Word and the Spirit that gives to the world its life and meaning.

Grant to all of us, O Lord, that by the power of the Holy Spirit, we may become so conscious of the gratuity of your presence and of your gifts that our relationships with our fellowmen will also become signs of your gracious presence and expressions of our gratitude and generosity.

2. *The presence of the Word Incarnate*

The world is like a great temple in which God, creator and artist, Lord and Father, is present. Our admiration should be unceasing, for the more we adore God in his wonderful presence to the world, the more we are astounded.

And wonder of wonders! The Word that dwelt with the Father, in whom all things are made, wants to be present in the world as our brother. He who is the light and the life of all life, the Word whose glory is proclaimed by all things, is present to us as one of us. 'So the Word became flesh; he came to dwell among us, and we saw his glory, such a glory as befits the Father's only Son, full of grace and truth' (Jn 1:14). He who makes visible his majesty and divinity in all of his creation, now makes visible and tangible to us his love, through Christ, Emmanuel, God-with-us. 'No one has ever seen God; but God's only Son, he who is nearest to the Father's heart, he has made him known' (Jn 1:8).

God has created us to be sharers of his own love and joy. He made us in his image and likeness, that we should be able to share his love with each other, to communicate it to each other in significant words and by acts of justice, kindness and goodness. But the ultimate sign of his love is that he himself wants to share in our human joys, our sorrows, our hopes and our anguish. The Word which was with the Father before the world began is present to us as our brother, as our companion on our earthly pilgrimage. He, the perfect image of the Father, shows us what it means to live with the Father and to make visible his love.

The prototype of the presence of Jesus, Son of the Father, is the Holy Family in the home at Nazareth. The Saviour's coming finds ready and free response in Mary: 'Behold, I am the handmaid of the Lord'. She receives him who is her Lord, who will make himself the servant of God and man.

With unlimited faith and with joyous welcome for the presence of the Word Incarnate, Mary's whole life becomes a song of wonder and gratitude. She is so filled with joy that, in her loving visitation, she brings this joyous message wherever she goes. Christ's presence to her, and her responsive presence to him, become a sharing of his presence with everyone she meets.

In the house in Nazareth we find the most wonderful image and reality of co-presence, because there we have the ideal reciprocity of consciousness. The joy of Mary and Joseph in

Jesus' presence opens a whole new vision to them, and through their grateful and loving presence to him they contribute to his wonderful growth in wisdom and graciousness as he advances in age.

Is it too much to think that Christ's unique experience of the heavenly Father's love is made possible to his human nature, at least partially, by his experience of Mary's and Joseph's love? They, in turn, seeing in the intimacy of their daily life the goodness and graciousness of Jesus, grow in their own understanding of the infinite love of the holy God.

In that home, Jesus hears about the great prophecies of the second Isaiah about the Servant Messiah, and thus the consciousness of being sent as servant to the world grows deeper and deeper within him. At the same time, Mary and Joseph, through their experience of Jesus' humanity, gentleness, obedience and desire to serve, gain a totally new understanding of these prophecies and a deeper understanding of every word of scripture.

Mary is present to Jesus not only as a loving mother but also as a mirror-image of him who is servant. For Mary is not like some of the relatives who want to take hold of Jesus and make him their own prophet. In the most crucial moments of his life as servant and prophet, Mary is present to him. It is as if her trustful word, 'They have no wine left' awakens in Jesus the already present trust in the Father who would always hear him. And her thoughtful care for her neighbour becomes a part of the creativity of Jesus, the friend of all people.

Under his cross, Mary's humble and trustful presence is the most eloquent witness of faith, and evokes in Jesus the most compassionate presence. Suffering does not close him within himself. Through his loving attention in the midst of his pain — 'Mother, there is your son' — Mary will be, for his disciple, a quasi-sacrament, a wonderful sign of the loving presence of Jesus himself. The beloved disciple, who took Mary into his home, shares with her the experience of Christ's faithful presence to the last moment (cf. Jn 16:26-27).

✚ We praise you, Mary, with Elizabeth, for your faith and for the welcome and loving attention you gave to your son, our brother, Jesus Christ. You loved him as your son and adored him as your Lord. For many years you had the great privilege of living in his intimate presence, and you were always present to him as mother, as disciple, as servant. Pray for us, that we may learn to rejoice in Jesus' presence and honour his name, Emmanuel.

Heavenly Father, we praise you, we love you, we render thanks to you for having made so wonderfully visible your own love through the presence of your only begotten Son, our Lord, Jesus Christ.

Send forth your Spirit and cleanse us, that with a pure heart we may recognize the presence of your beloved Son and Servant, Jesus Christ, with us and among us. Let us experience your own loving presence to us and to the whole world. And make us a truthful sign of your presence to our fellowmen.

3. Christ's call to his presence and an imperfect response

By his invitation, 'Follow me', Christ calls his disciples to be present to him. It is not only a word; it is the attractive power of Christ's person and his love that calls these men to him. When he repeats the same invitation to the same men — John, James and Peter — it is, each time, a new grace and a further call to a more intimate friendship.

But though Jesus is always present to his disciples with his love and his healing patience, they do not always respond with their attention to him. They are absent-minded, still partially the prisoners of their own plans and desires.

On the way to Jerusalem, when Jesus reveals himself as the Servant Messiah who will suffer and die for his friends, they do not really listen; they are still absorbed in their own illusions. Instead of asking the Master to help them to understand what he has been saying, the disciples lag behind, talking among themselves. When, in the evening, Jesus asks them, 'What were you arguing about on the way?' they keep silence 'because, on the way, they had been discussing who was the greatest' (Mk 9:30-34). They had kept at a distance because they could not discuss before the Master what they had in mind: honour and power. They did not want him to hear them and correct them.

Mark relates another striking instance of the disciples' non-presence to the Master. Having gathered the twelve together, Jesus told them openly about what would happen to him. 'We are now going to Jerusalem', he said, 'and the Son of man will be given up to the chief priests... He will be mocked and spat upon, flogged and killed; and three days afterwards, he will rise again' (Mk 10:32-34). Incredibly, when he had told them this, James and John, the sons of Zebedee, approached him to ask about their own career. 'Grant that we may sit in state with you, one at your right and the other at your left'. Jesus answered, 'You do not understand what you are asking' (Mk 10:37).

Peter, who had already experienced the divine presence of Christ and had confessed, 'You are the Messiah, the son of the living God' (Mt 16:16), was nevertheless not present to Jesus as a listening disciple when Jesus said plainly that he was to be put to death. Peter tried to impose his own way on the Master. 'He took him by the arm and began to rebuke him: "Far be it from you. No, Lord, this shall never happen to you"' (Mt 16:22). But Jesus could not accept this kind of invading presence. To be truly present and acceptable to the Lord, Peter would have to change. 'Jesus turned and said to Peter, "Away with you, Satan, you are a stumbling block to me, for you do not mind the things of God but those of men' (Mt 16:23).

Even at the last supper when Jesus foretold his deepest humiliation — that he would be betrayed by one of his disciples — they again talked of careers and self-importance. 'Then a jealous dispute broke out among them about who should rank highest' (Lk 22:24).

When Jesus was captured, Peter tried to urge him into combat by drawing his own sword and attacking the servant of the high-priest. When Jesus rebuked him and refused to fight, Peter still followed him; but later he could swear, 'I do not know that fellow', as Jesus was being shamefully led away and ill-treated. Yet Jesus remained present to Peter; he was waiting for his final conversion. 'And the Lord turned and looked straight at Peter, and Peter remembered the Lord's words, "Tonight, before the cock crows, you will have disowned me three times". And Peter went out and wept bitterly' (Lk 22: 60-62).

✝ O Lord, so often I have acted just as your disciples did. You have called me to your intimate friendship with the words 'Follow me', and I have lived my whole life with you, since you are always with me. But so often I have not listened to you; I did not want to know you as the humble servant of God and man, but preferred my own illusions. Therefore I have not always been present to you, and did not find my full joy in your presence. Forgive me, O Lord. Look mercifully on me as on Peter. Make me docile and humble, so that, with you, I can be a humble servant of the Father and of all people.

4. *The presence of the risen Lord*

Christ, the risen Lord, meets his disciples and reveals himself to them in his glory. It is not merely a subjective spiritual experience but is Christ himself who is the Encounter and who, by the power of the Holy Spirit, awakens his friends to the discovery of his presence. The Lord is present before the disciples see him and recognize him, but his presence is never unreal or passive; it is always the active, dynamic presence of him whom they have known and loved for years, graciously awakening and calling them to meet him and to be with him.

The main focus of the event of the resurrection in the four gospels, especially in that of St John, seems to me to be on this gradual discovery of Christ's presence. It is central to our faith that we truly believe that Christ is risen, but it is also important to understand the growth of our own faith in which we discover, more and more, what it means to live with Christ, the risen Lord.

Early on Easter morning, while it was still dark, Mary Magdalene, whose grateful love for Jesus had made her a new person, comes to the tomb. She is truly seeking Christ, although she hopes only to find his dead body. When she sees that the stone has been moved from the entrance, she is shocked and runs to find Peter and the beloved disciple, John. 'They have taken the Lord from his tomb', she cries, 'and we do not know where they have laid him' (Jn 20:2). Overcome by anxiety, disillusion and the pain of loneliness, she weeps, even when she meets the two angels who come to comfort her. And when she turns round, her tear-filled eyes do not recognize Jesus who is standing there. He asks, 'Why are you weeping? Who is it you are looking for?' And she, thinking he is the gardener and that he may have taken care of the body, answers, 'If it is you, sir, who removed him, tell me where you have laid him and I will take him away' (Jn 20:15). One day she will understand the word Jesus had spoken: 'I am the vine and my Father is the gardener' (Jn 15:1). She will no longer cling to the past, but recognize that Christ is life.

Then Jesus speaks one word. He calls Mary by her name. And this is the peak experience that brings to fulfilment all that Mary has experienced of Jesus during his earthly life. She turns to him and says, 'Rabbuni' — my Master. And she believes with all her heart in Christ's presence, in his resurrection. Yet when the Holy Spirit will be given in fullness, she will discover new and ever greater dimensions of the depth, the height, the length and the breadth of his loving presence.

This seems to be the meaning of Jesus' words, 'Do not cling to me for I have not yet ascended to my Father; but go to my brothers and tell them that I am now ascending to my Father and your Father, my God and your God' (Jn 20:17).

Through the strength and joy of her faith in the risen Lord, Mary Magdalene becomes an apostle to the apostles. 'I have seen the Lord', she rejoices; and she gives them his message, not only in words but by her whole life renewed by faith.

✛ I praise you, Lord Jesus, for the power of your loving presence to Mary Magdalene and to many who, like her, were sinners. Your coming and your presence during your earthly life, and even more after your resurrection, reveals the new creation in your disciples.

Let me, O Lord, know you and recognize your presence more and more deeply, so that like Mary Magdalene I may be able to be a messenger of your love and your life to my brothers and sisters, and encourage them on their way to discover you and to believe in you.

Lord, we are so often like Mary Magdalene. We do seek you but, as it were, only your body. We cling to traditions and formulas, and are disturbed if something is to be changed. Help us to find you, the risen Lord, you who are Life, so that our faith can become more radiant. Help us especially to discern your living presence in this moment of our history, and to accept its challenge.

5. 'Stay with us; for evening will come'

The appearance of the risen Lord to the two disciples on the way to Emmaus (Lk 24 : 13-33) is a kind of phenomenology of the crisis of faith among many of today's Catholics. Some had believed in a triumphalistic Church which must therefore be always right. When the Church was an absolute monopolist of truth, everything outside of our tent was considered to be only darkness. For others, faith was primarily an assurance that everything would be all right; God would preserve them from suffering and disappointment. Their faith is shaken because things went differently.

The two disciples whom Jesus meets on the way to Emmaus had enthusiastically followed Jesus of Nazareth. They had recognized in him 'a prophet powerful in speech and action before God and the whole people'. But, like so many others, they had expected a powerful messiah who would glorify Israel: 'We were hoping that he was the man to liberate Israel'.

With Jesus' crucifixion this kind of faith and hope had to collapse. And yet, there was in their faith also something more truthful: they loved Jesus. They recognized him as a man of God, and finally they remembered his word that after three days he would rise from the tomb. Also, they had kept in contact with those whose faith had already accepted Christ the Servant, whom the Father had glorified. Before they could have faith in the resurrection, they had to accept this divine design, according to which the Messiah is Servant, the One who bears the burden of all. 'Was the Messiah not bound to suffer before entering into his glory?'

Though it is difficult for them to understand and accept this message, they do ponder the words of scripture; they do listen now to what Jesus had told them during his earthly life; and they keep seeking with all their hearts. They pray, 'Stay with us, for evening draws on'.

Faith is a journey on which Christ is our hidden companion who gradually reveals himself. If we keep seeking sincerely, and praying, we are truly on the road of salvation and, time and again, will experience what the disciples experienced on the way to Emmaus: 'Did we not feel our hearts on fire as he talked to us on the road and explained the scriptures to us?'

For the disciples, the peak experience of faith happens when Jesus sits with them at table, takes bread and says the blessing, breaks the bread and offers it to them. Jesus is then truly their companion who finds a full response in awareness and gratitude. So, too, does the faith of many Christians experience the greatest breakthrough, the highest fulfilment, at the Eucharistic table, where they experience a community of faith gathered around the altar, listening to the word of God, joyously responding, and sharing Christ's Body and his peace.

As for Mary Magdalene, so for the two disciples, faith is a joyous and grateful acceptance of Christ's coming, of his gracious presence, and therefore of the mission of bringing the good news to others by word and life. This is, and will always be, the very heart of evangelization. Those who have found the risen Lord and who hear him with a sincere heart will be witnesses of his saving presence.

✚ Lord, look graciously on those whose faith is shaken: who, because of a certain kind of education and environment, were looking for a triumphalistic Church of unchanging formulations and traditions and had wrong expectations about you. Have mercy on those whose superficial faith is shaken. Be their companion on their difficult road, and help them to put their faith in you, Christ, who has suffered, was crucified, and has died for us. Then they too will experience the power and joy of your resurrection.

Lord, we do believe. Help us where our faith falls short.

6. *Peter meets the faith and love of John*

Peter sincerely loved and venerated his Master; he had come to faith in his divine power. But he had not yet come to full faith in the mystery of the Servant Messiah. The kind of expectations that were mixed up in his faith confused him. Jesus had chosen his way as the man of suffering, against Peter's protest; but he prayed for Peter: 'For you I have prayed, that your faith may not fail; and when you have come to yourself, you must lend strength to your brothers' (Lk 22:32).

Before his final conversion Peter was, in a way, a classical representative of an earthly messianism which had darkened the hope of Israel and hindered a great part of it from accepting

Jesus. The same kind of messianism has also been the greatest temptation within the Catholic Church.

Long before Boniface VIII asserted the direct power of the popes over all earthly realities, Peter had invented the theory of the two swords. He wanted to force Christ to be the kind of Messiah and the kind of national hero he wanted. Not only conservative popes, but also the most extreme liberals, have again and again fallen into the same confusion.

That same confusion exists today, and no less in one camp than in another. For some, faith is reduced to a 'social gospel'. For others it is *Kulturchristentum*, appreciated only in so far as it seems to be a part of the culture and allows a certain cultural advantage. For still others for whom revolution is 'in', Jesus is no more than the prophet for the kind of revolution they want. All these have in common Peter's self-importance and an arrogant self-trust that dares to appropriate Jesus for the particular messianic role he wants him to play.

With the collapse of Peter's wrong self-trust and of his illusion about the Messiah's mission, his faith is badly shaken. But the moment of his deepest misery was also a new beginning; for the Lord did not abandon him. Jesus had directed him to strengthen the faith of his brethren, and in his anxiety Peter needed to find help in John, the beloved disciple. After his terrible behaviour could he be sure of John's affection? Would he dare to seek him? But since John had seen the beloved Master turn to Peter in infinite compassion, he could not turn away from Peter. Or perhaps John had already been looking for Peter, fearing that he might fall into despair. In either case, when Mary Magdalene goes to find Peter, she finds these two men together.

John then not only outruns Peter by the strength of his faith but also graciously waits for him, encouraging him to follow on the road to faith. In the next chapter (Jn 21:7), we see him again in this role: 'The disciple whom Jesus loved said to Peter, "It is the Lord!" ' Jesus himself reveals the power of his resurrection to Peter by meeting him; but it is through the help of the loving disciple that Peter recognizes Christ the Servant and becomes a believer, a humble servant capable of strengthening the faith of his brothers.

All that the Bible says about the road to faith in the risen Lord is written for our own edification: to show us how we should help each other. 'With all this in view, you should try your best to supplement your faith with virtue, virtue with knowledge, knowledge with self-control, self-control with gratitude, gratitude with piety, piety with brotherly kindness, and brotherly kindness with love. These are gifts which, if you possess and treasure them, will keep you from being either useless or barren in the knowledge of our Lord, Jesus Christ' (2 Peter 1:5-8).

Especially in this present crisis of faith we need each other. We need the community of believers. Like Peter, we have the mission to strengthen the faith of our brothers and sisters, to be for each other messengers of peace and of faith in the risen Lord.

I do not think that we should assess the present crisis of faith only negatively. It is and can be a time of favour, a call to deepen our faith and to keep it pure by discerning better what is abiding truth and what are time-bound expressions. Then, when we look into its depths and discover new and challenging dimensions of faith, it will be an indication of Christ's presence with us.

It is true that our Lord also challenges and blames us — 'How dull you are, how slow to believe!' (Lk 24:25). But he does not condemn us; he helps us and will remain with us if we ask him insistently enough, 'Lord, abide with us'.

✛ O Lord, Jesus Christ, I believe that you are risen and that you are our Saviour and the Lord of the whole world. I believe that you are seeking me, that you are always present to me if only I make myself present to you. Send forth your Spirit, that he may purify my heart and open my eyes to your coming.

Give me friends in the community of believers. Let me experience the divine *milieu* of prayerful people, so that we can help each other to discover the dimensions and the bliss of your presence. Make us vigilant, O Lord, for your coming.

7. *The presence of Christ to his Church*

The risen Lord does not leave his disciples alone. Before he ascends to the Father, he promises them that they will be baptized by the power of the Holy Spirit (Acts 1:5). The coming of the Spirit will make them messengers of the good news and witnesses of the divine Master. 'But you will receive power when the Holy Spirit comes upon you; and you will bear witness to me in Jerusalem and all over Judea and Samaria, and away to the ends of the earth' (Acts 1:8). He also promises them his abiding presence. 'And be assured I am always with you to the end of time' (Mt 28:20).

The presence of Christ to his Church guarantees her indefectibility and vitality. However, this presence of the risen Lord is firmly linked with the task assigned to the Church, of proclaiming the good news of his death and resurrection and being a witness by her faith. The indefectibility is not an inherent quality which the Church can simply possess as a self-conscious institution. It is a gift that is always guaranteed by the divine Bridegroom, but the Church receives it only to the extent that she puts all her trust in him, lives in his presence, puts his gospel into practice, and gives witness to her faith through her love and justice for the sake of the life of the world.

The Church is holy, catholic and apostolic through Christ's undeserved presence and her own trust in him and her surrender to him. The community of believers is truly infallible when she teaches, by word and practice, that we cannot believe in one God, the Father, without loving all his children; that we cannot be true Christians and believers in the one Lord and Saviour, Jesus Christ, without a saving and healing love for all people; that we are true adorers of the Holy Spirit only if we consider all the gifts we have received as a sacred commitment to use them for the benefit of all.

Christ has given the promise of his saving and life-giving presence, not to a sedentary Church, not to an establishment satisfied with itself, but to a pilgrim Church which is willing to walk with him, to be watchful for his coming, and to bring the good news to all people by truthful witness as well as by word.

The presence of Christ to his Church becomes a visible and credible sign through the Church's watchfulness, her lively prayer, her trust in the Lord, and through her renouncing all forms of typically human power and any type of security complex that could lead her to compromise her authenticity as his messenger. The Lord's presence in his Church cannot be separated from the Church's humble prayer, 'Abide with us, O Lord', and her readiness: 'Here I am, send me'.

✛   O Jesus Christ, send your Holy Spirit to your Church and to all of us, your disciples, that we may put all our faith and trust in you and be converted to your gospel, put it into practice, and be your messengers and witnesses during all our life. Free us from that deceitful activism which leads people to put their trust in themselves and in all too human means.

Let our highest and most urgent desire be to spread your gospel and make your loving presence known to all. Give to each of us the blessing of a community of salvation that helps us to discover joy, strength of faith and trust in you.

Let us be rooted, O Lord, not in human traditions alone but in a community of faith that gives us the experience of your living presence in this, our own time in the history of salvation.

You are the Master, Lord, and you have called us. We answer, 'Lord, here we are. Send us'.

8. *The presence of Christ in the Eucharist*

The summit of the presence of the risen Lord and the Holy Spirit is the Eucharistic celebration. The Eucharist is the great mystery of faith in which Christ speaks to us by giving himself to us as the bread of eternal life. He proclaims his presence: 'I am here in your midst, I who died for you and live for you. I want to live in you and make you testimonies of my love and of my life'.

Christ is present in his word; he himself is the good news for us. Whenever we are open to the grace of the Holy Spirit in a community of believers, united in Christ who is our hope, ready to receive his word and to act on it, we discover anew that Christ's word is, for us, 'spirit and life' (Jn 6:63).

The whole Eucharistic celebration is a word and a gift of life that aims at our total conversion, our complete transformation in the Lord. The Eucharist is infinitely more than a memorial of past events. It is the Word Incarnate who reminds us of the past events that become a present reality for the believer. Christ, who died for us, is risen for us and has sent us the Spirit, is with us and proclaims that he will always be with us on our road until he comes in glory. He wants to make us sharers in the history of salvation by transforming us so that we can be co-revealers of his love for all whom we meet.

Christ's presence in the Eucharist, through his living word and under the species of bread and wine, is not separated into two entities. We distinguish two different aspects but they are one reality: Christ meeting us, speaking to us here and now, revealing to us, by his self-giving love, the final meaning of all the events of the history of salvation. He who comes to us under the species of bread and wine is, himself, the bread of life who gives life to the world so that we and the world may live in him, with him and through him.

The Eucharistic presence of Christ is the strongest, the most miraculous and the most effective presence in this world. It is Christ's presence, in the power of the Holy Spirit, who has anointed him to become the ransom for all people and who has raised him from the dead. When Christ meets us in the power of the Spirit, whom he bestows on us, we can receive this wonderful gift with thanks and praise, and respond by entrusting ourselves wholeheartedly to him, to become his witnesses to the ends of the earth.

It is through the Spirit that we can have living faith, acting in love. The prophetic word of Jesus is fulfilled in those who open themselves to the Spirit and celebrate the Eucharist with faith: 'If anyone is thirsty let him come to me; whoever believes in me, let him drink. Streams of living water shall flow out from within him' (Jn 7:38).

Only through the power of the Holy Spirit does the Eucharistic celebration become for us a peak experience in which we reach full reciprocity of consciousness. Through the Spirit, who is the self-giving love between the Father and the Son, we receive in the Eucharist a share in the love of the Son for the Father and the Father for the Son. Thus we receive the greatest gift, Christ himself, and we too can give ourselves totally to him and to his mission.

When Christ foretold the Eucharist, 'Whoever eats my flesh and drinks my blood possesses eternal life and I will raise him up on the last day' (Jn 6:55), many of his disciples demurred and left him, because his words made no sense to them. Jesus reminds them, then, of the gift of the Spirit: 'Does this shock you? What if you see the Son of man ascending to the place where he was before? The Spirit alone gives life; the flesh is of no avail; the words which I have spoken to you are both spirit and life' (Jn 6:61-63).

It is only through the Holy Spirit that Jesus is the Bread of life, available for all, ready to be eaten by all who need him and it is only by the same Holy Spirit that we ourselves, filled with gratitude for this greatest of gifts, can be ready to abandon ourselves to Christ and to follow him as servants of our brethren.

Clearly, then, we cannot say, as a certain school of Calvinists do, that Christ is 'only spiritually' present in the Eucharist. Yet I have heard a Presbyterian scholar say that this word 'only' must absolutely be dropped; for it is an insult to the risen Lord and to the Spirit to say 'only spiritually'. And he concluded, 'We can say that Christ is spiritually present if we mean that he is present by the power of the Holy Spirit, and that this is the most real, the most active, and the most demanding form of presence of the risen Lord'.

Since Christ, by the power of the Holy Spirit, gives nothing less than his life-giving body and blood in order to transform us into faithful people of the covenant, we can trust that the Spirit also gives us the strength and courage to give nothing less than ourselves for Christ and for his kingdom.

Christ is present in the Eucharistic banquet. He has chosen as symbol of his covenant presence, the family meal. He is present with that love of the covenant that calls all people to membership in his family. We can therefore be guests at his table and receive the blood of the covenant truthfully only if we are willing to become one in him. We cannot reach that reciprocity of consciousness with Christ, which is the aim of the Eucharist, unless we share Christ's love with our neighbour, first with those who are with us at the table, and then with all others, since Christ has shed the blood of the covenant for us and for all mankind.

Christ's presence in the Eucharist is infinitely dynamic. It is a divine energy that builds up and makes indispensible the unity of the disciples of Christ. To receive Christ truthfully in Holy Communion is to confirm again our readiness to be an active and ever more constructive member of his mystical Body.

When the Lord encounters us in the Eucharist, he wants to unite every fibre of our life with himself. It is a Communion of life and love. And since he offers himself as the living Bread for the life of the world, we receive, with his body, also the mission to live in that co-operative harmony which helps the world to believe that Christ is sent by the Father to call all people to oneness. When we receive his body in faith, we become his body, and thus witnesses to the Lord of the world who wants to make the world a divine *milieu*.

It is important but not sufficient to realize that the Eucharistic presence opens to us the dimensions of Christ's presence in and through the community of faith, hope and love, a presence that means final solidarity, the reciprocity of the consciousness of all men with Christ. It is not only this new horizon that we are able to understand through the Eucharistic presence of the Lord; we are also able to understand in a new way that whenever two or three meet in his name, he is in their midst.

✝ I thank you, Lord, with all my heart because the memory of your incarnation, passion, death, resurrection, and ascension to heaven is not only an account that comes to us from past history. You yourself come graciously to remind us that you were born for us, you have suffered for us, you are alive for us. You want to live in us and with us in order to continue, through us, your saving love for all people in all time.

Lord, I believe that you are the life of our life, the strength of our strength, and the road of salvation.

I thank you, Lord, that our thanksgiving is not ours alone but is united with the thanks and praise you have offered to our heavenly Father. Grant, by the Holy Spirit, that we may always celebrate the memory of your incarnation, passion, death, resurrection and ascension with such great faith, joy, and gratitude, that all our life becomes, in union with you, praise and thanksgiving to the Father. And help us to honour the name of the Father by being one with your redemptive love for all the world.

9. *The presence of Jesus in the Blessed Sacrament*

Once the priest has spoken the Lord's words over the bread during the Eucharistic celebration, 'This is my body, given for you', it will never be simply bread, but a sign of Christ's abiding presence and of his desire always to be available as the Bread of life for the world.

The presence of Jesus in the tabernacle is a unique manifestation of his loving concern for all who need him. For the sick and the dying he is always ready to be the Bread of life.

For the troubled and weary, and for all who come to him for enlightenment or just to be with him, to praise him and express their thanks to him, he is abiding presence, comfort, peace and joy.

It is not for man to give to the consecrated bread the signification of Christ's presence; it is he himself, to assure us of his abiding presence. He is truly there for us, but it depends on us whether we open ourselves to awareness and to receive his blessing. The Lord invites us constantly to find our repose in him, our best friend.

I do not assert that the practice of the visit to the Blessed Sacrament is indispensable for salvation, but I do not hesitate to recommend it wholeheartedly. The gift of the Lord in the Blessed Sacrament refreshes our memory. It is a contemplative and quiet celebration of his dynamic presence, which deepens our gratitude and our friendship and helps us to celebrate the next Eucharist with even greater love and joy.

We meditate before the tabernacle on what the Lord has told us in the Eucharist: that to render thanks always and everywhere is the way to salvation. And, in his presence, we test again and again the truthfulness of our life: whether we are acting towards our brethren in a spirit of thankfulness befitting the Eucharistic gift we have received.

If we were to seek Christ in the tabernacle and fly to him only because we do not like to be with people, we should be unable to find him truly. It would be an alienation. But if we understand his loving presence, and find our rest and peace before him, we can also better realize that Christ is present wherever two or three are gathered in his name.

When we experience a personal encounter with Christ — 'Thou and I' — we never forget the dimension of 'we', because the Eucharistic presence is always a reminder of Christ's rallying call, whereby he calls us all together in the communion of saints.

✢ I thank you, my Lord and my Saviour, my friend and brother, for your silent yet eloquent presence in the Blessed

Sacrament. You are always waiting for me in this abiding sign of the new and everlasting covenant.

Lord, awaken in me such a spirit of gratitude that I shall gladly accept your invitation to find rest and peace in your presence, so that my life can radiate peace and graciousness to my fellowmen. Lord, let me learn in your presence that kind of thankfulness which becomes generosity and appreciation of the love of my fellowmen.

10. Christ's coming in baptism

When Jesus was baptized in the Jordan, his meeting with all the others who were baptized at the same time was full of import. He joined them as the Man for all people, in a wonderful solidarity. 'And while he was praying, heaven opened and the Holy Spirit descended on him in bodily form as a dove; and there came a voice from heaven, "You are my Son, my beloved; on you my favour rests" ' (Lk 3 : 22).

To those who know that they are sinners and are baptized in the hope of, and readiness for, conversion, the coming of Christ becomes an epiphany, a revelation of the Holy Spirit and of the love of the heavenly Father for his Son who is ready to bear the burden of all mankind.

When he comes into our life, the Father's love for him and for us becomes visible. On the cross, when Jesus is baptized again in his own blood, the blood of the covenant, he is near, with an infinite love, not only to his mother Mary and the beloved disciple, but to all of us sinners, when he prays for those who have crucified him and welcomes to his kingdom the thief at his side who puts his final trust in him.

By our baptism we partake of the baptism of Christ. He himself baptizes us by the Spirit, thus calling us into the covenant sealed by his blood. Christ not only speaks a welcoming word of love and power during the baptism; he meets the baptized. He wants to abide with him and to transform him so that his life can mirror Christ's own solidarity and all-embracing love for his brothers and sisters.

The sacrament of confirmation completes baptism. Christ was not baptized by water alone but in water, in his blood, and by the Spirit. In confirmation he comes again to baptize us with the Spirit.

His presence with those who are baptized reveals itself more and more as they grow towards a full maturity that looks on everything in a perspective of gratitude. When we have learned to make our decisions and to orient our lives around the prayer, 'What can I give to the Lord for what he has given me?', the happy awareness that Christ is with us in our daily lives becomes more and more intense.

Baptism and confirmation are decisive events, decisive moments of encounter with Christ. In them he comes, through his gifts and through his word, as a challenge to us to live fully and become more and more mature members of his holy people, in view of a new creation.

But it is not just at the moment of the reception of the sacrament that we meet Christ. He comes into our life to be with us and in us, and to awaken our consciousness to the wonder of his abiding presence and to gratitude for it.

To live according to the gifts of these sacraments means to help each other towards greater awareness of his being with us. It is in this perspective that we can understand when, in the language of the charismatic renewal, people speak about baptism in the Holy Spirit. They have not in mind a new sacrament, but through their experience as members of a community of faith, love and praise, they invite the Spirit so that the sacraments of baptism and confirmation may become a more conscious reality in their life.

In shared prayer we are aware of our being baptized by the Holy Spirit. If we pray with each other and for each other, that the Spirit may come upon us, and if at the same time we work to build up a divine *milieu* of Christian joy, hope, mutual respect and encouragement, then we are on the way to a full reciprocity of consciousness: we are experiencing more intimately the presence of Christ who has baptized us and continues to baptize us in the Holy Spirit. We open ourselves to him so that, with him, we can praise the Father and bear fruit in love for the life of the world.

✝ In awareness of the reality of our baptism and in gratitude for it, we praise you, Father, Lord of heaven and earth. We praise you because your Servant, Jesus Christ, wanted to be baptized with the crowd of humble people who knew that they were sinners. We thank you that, through baptism, you gather your people to make them one and holy.

We beg you, Father, to grant to your Church a deeper and deeper knowledge of what you mean by baptism: that infants should be baptized not only with water and words, but that they should be truly inserted into a community of believers, thus to experience the joy and strength of faith. Help us to build up that divine *milieu* in which we and our fellow Christians can more fully understand what baptism in the Holy Spirit means for us. Send us your Spirit, that our life may bear the fruits of the Spirit in kindness, gentleness, generosity, spontaneity, and creativity.

Assist people's effort in the charismatic renewal and in other prayer movements. Let their prayer and their lives bring to the whole Church the message that the Spirit is truly our life and our guide.

Come, Holy Spirit, cleanse us from our sins. Let us share in the joy of the risen Lord, and let our life be joined with him, so that we may always experience his nearness.

11. *The Lord's presence in the effective signs of reconciliation*

The heavenly Father's concern that none of the little ones should be lost is made evident in Christ's coming as the Good Shepherd (cf. Mt 18:14).

Every Christian who lives in union with Christ the Redeemer, the Good Shepherd, the Divine Physician, exercises a co-responsibility according to his special charism. We are all asked to be for each other a sign of reconciliation and an effective help in salvation. 'If your brother commits a sin, go and take the matter up with him alone, between yourselves, and if he listens to you, you have won back your brother' (Mt 18:16).

Whenever the saving event of fraternal correction and encouragement occurs, a particularly active presence of Christ is guaranteed, whether this help is offered by a Christian layman or laywoman, by a group of people, or by the assembly and those appointed to the ministry of reconciliation. We honour this reconciling presence by prayer, relying on God's grace: 'I tell you this: if two of you on earth agree about any request, it will be done for them by my Father in heaven; for if two or three have met together in my name, I am there among them' (Mt 18:19-20). From its context, this text is evidently related to fraternal correction by a brother or sister in Christ as well as to the reconciling effort of the official Church and her ministers.

By faith and grace we recognize the gratuitousness of redemption and the power of the Spirit, and our gratitude moves us to help one another, to strengthen one another, and to bear one another's burdens. 'If the Spirit is the source of our life, let the Spirit also direct our course. We must not be conceited, challenging one another to rivalry, jealous of one another. If a man should do something wrong, my brothers, on a sudden impulse, you who are endowed with the Spirit must set him right again, very gently. Look to yourself, each one of you: you may be tempted too; carry each other's troubles, and in this way you will fulfil the law of Christ' (Gal 5:25-6:2).

James, too, admonishes us: 'Be patient and stout-hearted, for the coming of the Lord is near. My brothers, do not blame one another for your troubles or you will fall under judgement. . . Confess your sins to one another and pray for one another, and then you will be healed, redeemed. A good man's prayer is powerful and effective' (James 5: 8-16).

Until the time of Albert the Great and Thomas Aquinas, fraternal correction, offered in a spirit of gentleness and in awareness that we all depend on God's patience and graciousness, followed by humble avowal of the fault and by prayer, was always considered as a kind of sacrament, a particular expression of the sacrament of divine forgiveness. This vision did not at all diminish the special role of the priest as a minister of reconciliation. In many parts of the Orthodox Church, for example in Russia, confession to holy lay persons is still practised and considered as a sacrament. If we experience in our daily life Christ's gracious presence by helping each other to overcome our limitations and faults, then we shall also come to a better understanding of the celebration of the Church's sacrament of reconciliation.

It is always Christ himself who comes and assures us of forgiveness, but he has chosen to do it ordinarily in a very visible and effective way through the ministry of the Church.

In the sacrament of reconciliation we meet the priest who, through his charism and mission, is truly a sign of the presence of the Good Shepherd, of the Divine Physician. We see, then, the essence of this sacrament, that it is not so much our own endeavour, but rather Christ who, through grace, the mercy of the heavenly Father, and his own gentle presence and healing power, calls us to the humble avowal of our sins and the re-direction of our life towards his goodness. Christ himself, through the healing kindness of our neighbour and the consoling message of the commissioned messenger of reconciliation, kindles in us a new courage and the desire to respond to his call to follow him and to carry out our share in the redemptive mission of the Church.

✛ We pray, in the spirit of the ancient Roman liturgy cele-
brated on Maundy Thursday and called, 'public reconciliation of
sinners':

It is right and fitting, it is a sign of your gracious presence
and a way of salvation, to render thanks always and everywhere
to you, all-merciful God.

When men first fell into sinfulness and alienation, you did
not abandon them. As a sign of salvation, you gave to Adam
and Eve sons like Abel and Seth who knew how to invoke your
name and to praise your goodness.

When Cain slaughtered his brother, you yourself made a sign
on his face that slaughter should not go on.

And when the earth was flooded with sin, you saved Noah,
his family, and all the species of animals out of the chaos of
waters.

You made Joseph, whom his brothers had sold into slavery, a
wonderful sign of forgiveness and reconciliation.

And when your people in slavery called to you for liberation,
you led them out of Egypt, through the Red Sea, through the
desert and over the Jordan into the promised land.

You taught the prostitute Rahab to show mercy to the
ambassadors of your people, and in turn you taught your people
to show mercy to her.

When the anointed King David offended you gravely by
taking another man's wife and killing the husband, you sent him
the prophet to shake his conscience and make him aware of his
crime. And when he showed repentance, you made known to
him your mercy and reconciled him.

At the appointed time you sent Jesus Christ, your Son, and
made him the great sacrament of reconciliation, the Good
Shepherd who seeks the lost sheep, the Divine Physician who
heals the sick, the source of living water who, by the power of
the Holy Spirit, can raise to life those who were dead in their
sins.

Therefore with the angels and saints, with all those who, throughout history, have been messengers of your peace and ministers of reconciliation we commit ourselves to the same mission, to be signs of your merciful presence, and thus to praise your name.

12. *The nearness of the Lord to the priest and through the priest*

The priest is called to be, above all, a man of prayer. By his mission, he is a hearer of the word of God who treasures it up in his heart and ponders it. He is one who has made it the main purpose of his life to be an adorer of God in spirit and in truth, and to help all the priestly people of God to abide in the word of the Lord, to pray, and to find a synthesis between faith and life, to the honour of the one God and Father.

Since the priest is sent to speak not in his own name but in the name of the Lord, to make known the Lord's loving presence, the first condition for his life's fulfilment is that he should live in the deepest possible union with the One who sends him. Only in this way can he live his special charism to make known to his brothers and sisters that the Lord is near.

To be an effective and attractive sign of God's presence to mankind, the priest must be rich in the qualities of sympathy and human understanding. To the very best of his ability, he has to acquire a wide-ranging and profound knowledge of man and of the world in which he lives.

The relationship of the priest with his fellow believers is by no means a one-way street. It is through the Christian community, through his parents and his friends, that he learns how to pray, how to grow in the knowledge and the joy of faith. And in order to be a sign of God's loving presence, he himself needs the love, the kindness, patience and understanding of his fellow Christians.

We pray to Christ, the prophetic high-priest:

✛ We thank you, O Lord, because you inspire men and women to dedicate themselves wholly to your gospel and to be for us signs of your own total consecration to the gospel of our heavenly Father.

Lord Jesus, we thank you for the priestly ministry that brings us into closer contact with you. Send your Church priests who are also prophets, who have experienced your holiness and your kindness, and are men of faith and hope from whom we can learn what it means to adore with you the Father in spirit and in truth.

13. *The presence of the Lord in matrimony*

God is love, the source of all goodness; and wherever we find true love, or even an imperfect love that is striving for greater fullness and truthfulness, there is God. There is a sign of his active presence and a path to him.

The sacrament of marriage is not only a blessed symbol of the covenant which God has offered mankind in Jesus Christ; it is also a visible and most effective sign of Christ's own loving presence in and with the husband and wife. On this point *The pastoral constitution on the Church in the modern world* is very explicit:

'Christ the Lord abundantly blessed this many-faceted love, welling up as it does from the fountain of divine love and structured as it is on the model of his union with the Church. For as God of old made himself present to his people through a covenant of love and fidelity, so does the saviour of man and the spouse of the Church come into the lives of married Christians through the sacrament of matrimony. He abides with them thereafter so that, just as he loved the Church and handed himself over on her behalf, the spouses may love each other with perpetual fidelity through a mutual self-bestowal' (*Gaudium et spes* 48).

The heart of sacramentality is always love that comes from God and leads to God. Everywhere and at all times, marriage has had the great sacramental value of keeping men and women from loneliness and from self-centredness, and of involving them in the long human history of a growing love and growing discernment of what deserves this noble name and what does not. Without this human experience of the love accumulated in the world through marriage and family, we should probably have no access, psychologically, to an understanding of what a sacrament is.

Matrimony is a sacrament not only for the husband and wife but also for their children and their fellowmen. The family is the indispensable living and life-giving cell of the Church, and therefore has a most active part in the on-going realization of God's covenant with mankind. Wherever Christians fully live this great covenant of faithful, creative, life-giving and generous love, they radiate joy and faith, and help their fellowmen to become more fully aware of how God comes wonderfully into our lives.

In marriage, human love achieves a unique reciprocity of consciousness through the mutual awareness and mutual appreciation of husband and wife, and their gratitude, encouragement and praise. As they become, through faith, increasingly conscious that their own love, their being united with each other, is a gift of God's love, a new dimension of reciprocity opens to them. They find that the more they love each other, the more they become conscious of and grateful for God's love for them.

The consciousness of Christ's healing presence in a truly Christian marriage not only encourages husband and wife to strive for a deeper and deeper love, but helps them to accept and to integrate their human failures and limitations into a perspective of trust in God's patient work in them.

For young couples one of the most challenging experiences comes when the early illusions have worn off and they have to learn to accept each other as they now experience them-

selves in daily life. This learning process will be most fruitful
if they keep in mind that they are not meant to be idols for
each other, and that they are not, themselves, the source or
the final goal of love, but are the channels through which
God's love flows out to each other, to their children, and to
all the world.

When they realize this, then they also realize that Christ
loves us human beings as we really are: he seeks us where we
are in order to transform us into masterpieces of his love, in
his own image and likeness. The awareness of this need for
gradual transformation in order to become ever more a 'sacrament', a visible sign of God's love, will lead the spouses to turn
to the Holy Spirit who alone can transform and renew their
hearts and increase their capacity to love.

When husband and wife humbly request and grant each other
forgiveness for faults and offences, and also ask their children
to forgive them when they have unjustly blamed or punished
them, then all together come to an awareness of the presence of
Christ, the healer and reconciler.

Married couples who accept their noble vocation to co-
operate with God's own creative love, will easily come to a more
profound awareness of the presence of God, Creator and
Redeemer. As they educate their children towards maturity, they
will be conscious that God himself is present in them and in
their children, to mould them in his image, so that they may
be, for the world, witnesses of his transforming love.

To be aware of the Lord's presence in their family life is,
in itself, prayer; but progress in awareness cannot be made without explicit prayer. Family prayer is a sign that the members
of the family truly believe in the Lord's nearness in their daily
joys, hopes and sorrows. There should be, however, not only
structured prayer but also the spontaneous sharing of expressions
of faith, hope, love and gratitude, in the various events of their
life.

Christian families who live consciously in God's presence
do not confine their love to their own homes; it overflows into

the outside world and into many hearts. They are always ready to give friendship to the lonely ones who, without free choice, are deprived of a home and the warmth of a family. And even the lives of those who, for the sake of the gospel, have chosen or accepted celibacy, are in many ways nourished and sustained by the love-witness of married couples, especially of their own parents who were, for them, the first witnesses of that life-giving love which comes from God and leads back to God.

✝ We thank you, Lord, for all the love, kindness and patience which your presence has structured into families all over the world and in all religions. We praise you for having made known the source and the goal of all this love to those who believe in you and live the covenant of love in your honour.

We beg you, Lord, to help those husbands and wives who are experiencing family difficulties. Teach them to love each other and to love and accept their children and draw them closer to you. Let them realize that you can, indeed, come into their life and strengthen them so that they can grow in redeemed and redeeming love.

To all the husbands and wives and parents whose love mirrors your own, grant full consciousness that you alone are the giver of this love, so that they will honour and praise you for it.

Lord, we ask you also to comfort and help those who are unable to build their own marriage and family, and for those who are abandoned and live a lonely life. Send them friends, kind and generous people who can become for them a sign of your loving presence.

And grant to those who, for your kingdom, have chosen a celibate life, the capacity to love you in such a way that they can join their love with your own for those who are particularly in need of it.

14. *The presence of Christ to the sick*

It is impressive to see how the sick gained trust and confidence whenever Jesus came. He was totally present to them with all his loving attention and the healing power of his kindness. Christ is ever present to all of us as the Divine Physician who heals us in our human weaknesses, but he wants to manifest his presence in a very special way to those who are suffering or sick.

It is through kind and good physicians, and nurses, and loving relatives and friends that the Lord makes the sick alert to his own compassionate and consoling presence with them. Even so, it may not mean too much to the sick person if the priest then rushes in and performs in routine fashion the rite of the anointing of the sick. But if he experiences the kindly presence of believers, or if some of his friends have prayed with him and helped him to understand the ultimate meaning of suffering and sickness, and then the priest comes with the same love, gentleness and concern, making known the love of the Divine Physician, the sacrament of the anointment of the sick has profound significance for the sufferer. At such a time, he or she can come truly to a peak experience of the presence of the Lord.

Again we have to remember that presence includes and awakens a reciprocity of consciousness. Not only does Christ want to be present to the sick person; he wants the person to be present to him, to unite himself and his suffering with the power of the paschal mystery. Christ comes in the sacrament to meet his suffering friends so that they can become truly aware of him, consciously turn to him, and allow him to insert their suffering into the saving event of his own death and resurrection.

We should all see our own role and mission of helping the sick, especially those who are facing death, by making them aware of Christ's redeeming presence with them on their way. When we do this we are one with Christ who, in the Viaticum, invites the believer to make himself ready for his final coming.

✛ We pray to you, Divine Physician, to illumine and strengthen all of us, and especially our doctors and nurses, and the friends and relatives of our sick brothers and sisters, so that we may be able to communicate to them the experience of your loving and healing care.

O Divine Physician, let us experience in the crucial moments of our life that you are near to us and that we can entrust ourselves to you. Strengthen our faith in your paschal mystery, in your passion and resurrection, so that those moments which are meaningless without you can receive, through your presence and our response to you, final meaning for us and for the salvation of the world.

15. *The presence of Christ in the fraternal community*

We are united in the name of Christ whenever and wherever we meet each other with the love that has its origin in God and points to him. Such an encounter mediates in us a growing awareness of the dynamic and active presence of God who is helping us to grow in our knowledge of him. 'Dear friends, let us love one another because love is from God. Everyone who loves is a child of God and knows God; but the unloving know nothing of God; for God is love' (1 Jn 4: 7-8).

Christ is the perfect and most evident sign of God's loving presence to men. His humanness and kindness united his disciples who, by nature and temperament, could not otherwise have become a community. In Christ and through him, all human persons and communities that manifest the harvest of the Spirit — gentleness, kindness, benevolence, respect, goodness, faithfulness, generosity — help their fellowmen to know God and to live consciously and gratefully in his presence. 'Though God has never been seen by any man, God himself dwells in us if we love one another; his love is brought to perfection within us' (1 Jn 4: 12).

Those who offer love to others and those who accept it in

readiness to respond are equally helped to come to a deeper and more pervading awareness that the Lord is present. If we love our brothers and sisters, refusing no one, and if we accept the signs of their goodness with appreciation, then we can believe truthfully and joyously that God lives in us.

If his love is in us and unites us among ourselves, then we know that the Lord is with us and in us. 'If anyone says "I love God", and hates his brother, he is a liar. If he does not love the brother whom he has seen, how can he love God whom he has not seen?' (1 Jn 4:20).

A profound friendship that has its source in God will always tend to point to him. When each friend, by his or her own presence and being, allows Christ to continue his loving presence with the other, then both will easily come to share with each other their experience of God's work in them, and will discover together the meaning of Christ's coming in all the daily events of their lives.

✝ We praise you, Father, because you have created all our brothers and sisters in your image and likeness, and because among our fellowmen there are those who are truly like you, who remind us of you by their love and kindness.

We thank you, O God, for the community of believers, for all those who share with us our hope to be with you, once for all, in the communion of saints.

Cleanse us by the power of your Spirit, so that we can truly be an image and likeness of you for each other, and become for all people a sign of your loving presence in this world.

16. *The coming of Christ in the poor*

Almost every page of scripture, beginning with the prophets and through the letters from John and James, tells us that the test of our love and a sign of the special presence of the Lord is the poor. 'But if a man has enough to live on and yet, when he sees his brother in need, shuts his heart against him, how can it be said that the divine love dwells in him?' (1 Jn 3:17).

The poor who put us to the test are not only those whose poverty is in material goods; they can equally be those who, because of a bad heredity and environment, are unable to love, and are therefore disagreeable, even nasty.

With infinite generosity, God has given us many signs and experiences of his loving presence. If, therefore, through the power of his Spirit, we are able to love the poor and the miserable, and yet refuse or neglect to help them or enrich them with generous and patient love, then we are refusing to welcome Christ who calls us and puts us to the test through them. If we are not willing to welcome him when he meets us in the person of the poor, in those who particularly need our love and our help, how can we find joy in the eucharistic presence of Christ, or receive him joyously in Holy Communion, or welcome him at the hour of our death?

In Russia, one hears the story of Pavlov, who tells his children that, on Christmas eve, Jesus will come to visit them. They are filled with excitement, and as the days go by, they ask their father again and again, 'How shall we know Jesus? What will he look like?' Pavlov answers each time, 'My dear children, pray. Pray each day, "Jesus, son of David, son of the living God, have mercy on me, that I may see and recognize you".'

The day before Christmas, when expectation is at its height, someone knocks at the door. Pavlov opens it immediately, and there stands a beggar, shabby, dirty, malodorous; yet Pavlov receives him as if he were a king. He washes him, anoints his sores, fits him with good clothes, then seats him at the table and serves him. At this moment, the children interrupt to ask once more, 'Father, when will Jesus at last come to visit us?' Pavlov weeps. 'My children, how often did I tell you and beg you to pray — and you are still blind?'

✝ O Jesus Christ, Emmanuel, you who are infinitely rich have come to us as one who is poor, in order to be near to us. And until your glorious final coming, you will meet us again and again in the disguise of the poor.

Come to us. Grant that through the power of your Spirit we may recognize and welcome you in our brother who needs our love, our respect and our help.

17. *The presence of the triune God to his friends*

When our life accords with faith, and our prayer is authentic, the consciousness of God's presence increases in us.

God is not only present around us as our Creator; he is in us and with us. He is closer to us than our own consciousness. When we live in his grace, and grow in our love for Christ, the presence of God is the blessed source of our inner joy and peace.

The triune God has his dwelling place with those who follow his Son as friends and faithful servants. Christ speaks of this presence in his farewell discourse. 'Anyone who loves me will heed what I say; then my Father will love him and we will come to him and make our dwelling with him' (Jn 14:23).

The Father and the Son come to us in the joy of the Spirit, who enables us to entrust ourselves to him. 'If you love me, you will keep my commandments; and I will ask the Father and he will give you another Advocate who will be with you forever — the Spirit of truth' (Jn 14:15-16).

If we are docile to the Holy Spirit, he will transform us into truthful sons and daughters of God. The total word that Christ has spoken to us through his incarnation, life, death and resurrection, will abide in us. And then the Father will hear us. 'If you dwell in me and my words dwell in you, ask what you will and you shall have it. As the Father has loved me, so I have loved you. Dwell in my love' (Jn 15:7-9).

The indwelling of the Holy Trinity in those who are justified by faith goes hand in hand with that fraternal love which makes us signs of God's presence to each other.

This deep and intimate indwelling of God is a source of joy and strength. It is also, sometimes, a burning and purifying fire by which God prepares us for an ever more profound and blissful experience of his presence. The painful experience of our sinfulness and weakness, and of our deep need for an ongoing conversion, prompt us to turn more decisively to the Lord, to put all our trust in him and to seek only him.

The closer we come to an intimate union with God, the more clearly we discern God's initiative. We see that everything we are and possess is his undeserved gift; but thus we also experience the urgent appeal that comes from this gratuitous love of the Lord. 'You have received the grace of God; do not let it go for nothing. God's own words are, "In the hour of my favour I gave heed to you; on the day of deliverance I came to your aid. The hour of favour has now come" ' (2 Cor 6: 1-2).

How great can our beatitude be even here on earth if we are fully responsive to God's gracious coming and docile to the Spirit who dwells in us.

✝ O merciful and loving God, I am confident that you have taken up your dwelling in my innermost being and that you will always be with me as my Father, my Friend, my Comforter.

I am deeply sorry that I have so often lived on a superficial level and wasted time with useless and vain thoughts. Even now, by giving attention to so many things that have no abiding value, I expose myself too often to the danger of forgetting your holy presence.

Grant, O Lord, that we may so celebrate the memorial of the paschal mystery that, through Communion with Jesus and through our fraternal unity, we may become always more aware of and grateful for your presence in us and with us.

Lord, make us holy. Lord, make us one. Keep us in your friendship and purify us, so that we shall become more worthy to be a dwelling place for you, our Father, our origin and our goal, and for your Son, Jesus Christ, and your Holy Spirit. Amen.

Chapter 3

PRAYER AND THEOLOGY

1. *Theology is prayer: prayer is theology*

Whoever wants to make a contribution to theology has to do hard and careful work, has to dedicate himself to painstaking scientific research in whatever fields may lead him to an ever better knowledge of God and man. He must submit himself to scientific method, must have a knowledge of languages and of the social and cultural context of scripture and later traditions. He needs intuition, a sense of synthesis and expertise in history, in order to assess the context in which the Church has worked out her doctrine and life, and thus distinguish the main-stream of divine tradition from ossified human traditions.

Obviously, then, to be a good theologian, piety alone does not suffice. Yet it has to be emphatically affirmed that the very heart of theology is prayer. It is an absolute condition for the theologian if he wants to be on the right wavelength in his endeavour. Prayer confronts him with the living God and gives to his study the quality of an act of faith.

Faith is the joyous, humble, grateful and adoring reception of God who reveals himself as our life and our saving truth. The primordial act of faith and theology is listening to God who speaks to us and reveals his love for us and for all mankind, and thus calls us to unity with himself and among ourselves.

Faith, theology and prayer require attention to all that God has revealed to man, but even more they require loving attention to God himself in his act of self-revelation. Whoever forgets God deprives his word and his action of their source of life, their gift of joy; they are no longer spirit and truth. One cannot possibly receive the word of God in a vital way without a grateful heart and trust in him. Furthermore, sincere and authentic listening to God presupposes the readiness to respond to him with one's whole being. In a specific Christian understanding, human life and morality constitute a total response to God, that can be fulfilled only to the extent that we bring the whole of our life home to him in faith.

A prayerful theologian manifests a radical readiness to hear the word of God and to respond to him in view of the salvation of all mankind. In other words, theology is an expression of the love of God and man, and a service of salvation.

God's word is ever active, ever creative, a redeeming light and energy, since God is present in his word and in whatever he does and communicates to us. Theology listens to him as he speaks in the ongoing creation and history of man. A theologian who is an adorer of God in spirit and truth can never forget that God reveals himself and his design of salvation, of peace and joy, in all his works, and above all, in his masterpiece, the human person, created in his image and likeness.

God is always present to us; he aways comes dynamically into our life, bringing his work gradually to fulfilment. This demands on our part constant attention and readiness to be his co-workers, co-creators, and co-revealers of his love. The theologian is called, with all his fellow Christians and even in a particular way, to grow in the knowledge and love of God so that he can be ever more a co-revealer of God in his ongoing creation and his act of redemption which renews the face of the earth and the hearts of men. Only in so far as he lives in the spirit of adoration and praise can he come to a comprehensive understanding of the sense of history. Without that spirit, the theologian will lack the necessary connaturality with the design and loving presence of God in history.

This is a point strongly stressed by Saint Thomas Aquinas: that all history is a living and active word of God, the history of the relationship between God and man. We are all inserted into, and involved in this powerful and ongoing word of revelation. God takes us seriously while he calls us to work with him. This gives stability and continuity to theology and to the theologian who, by constant attention to God's presence in human events, acquires an increasing awareness of being on the road with the Lord of history.

By its very vocation, theology is a vigilant, adoring and grateful attention to the redeeming presence of God in the world. It demands outstanding alertness in the dialogue between God and man. In Jesus Christ, true God and true man, there is the absolute reciprocity of persons: Jesus lives the perfect consciousness of his coming from the Father and returning to him. The love of the Father for all men shines forth in him as perfect humanness, perfect consciousness, in total response to this very love. By loving all mankind with the love of his Father, the Son of man reveals the Father to man.

The theologian enters the history of this reciprocity of consciousness only to the extent that he himself grows in awareness of God's presence in history here and now. In this awareness he can reach out from an understanding of the past to the dynamic of hope which promises the fullness of reciprocity. To speak properly to others about this event which is itself truth, he has to live intensely in the presence of God, Creator and Redeemer.

God's presence is a rallying call. When God calls men to himself, his word is at the same time a call to brotherhood. His name, 'Father', is hallowed when men are one in mutual respect, in love and justice. This is God's glory on earth. It is expressed also in the friendship of theologians among themselves and with their students. And this friendship is always meant for all those to whom the word of God is directed. A healthy theological community is not thinkable without foundation in a community of prayer which demonstrates its oneness in faith and in the loving concern of its members for one another.

A theology degenerates inevitably into Pelagianism when theologians imagine that they are able to say something reasonable and worthy of God without the active presence of the Holy Spirit. Theology demands complete awareness of our dependence on God's gracious presence; and this is not possible without unceasing prayer, humble and grateful openness to the grace of the Holy Spirit.

A theologian should also be fully aware of being 'a man with impure lips, living among people of impure lips' (Is 6 : 5). Theology itself, as an encounter with the holy God, will lead him to pray, 'Let your Holy Spirit come upon us and purify us'. This prayer is, in the oldest manuscripts, a part of the *Our Father* in the eleventh chapter of St Luke. Our theology is the more imperfect, fragmented and exposed to error, the less our heart is purified by the Spirit and by our response to him. Only 'the pure in heart shall see God' (Mt 5 : 8).

Christ has come to baptize us with the Spirit and with fire. It is the Holy Spirit who gives energy, enthusiasm and purity of intention to the theologian. No genuine theological work is possible without the experience of Moses and the other prophets. When Moses met God as a living fire, 'he covered his face for fear to look at God' (Ex 3 : 5-6). The prophet Isaiah came to know the purifying strength of the fear of God. 'One of the seraphim flew to me, holding an ember which he had taken with the thongs from the altar of God. He touched my mouth with it. "Now that this has touched your lips, your wickedness is removed, and your sin is purged" ' (Is 6 : 5-6).

This purifying experience leads man into the promised land of the knowledge of God. From it derives the authentic mission of the theologian. 'And I heard the voice of the Lord saying,

"Whom shall I send?" And I answered, "Here am I. Send me" ' (Is 6:8).

Of what value is a theologian who has never had the experience that Christ has come to bring fire on the earth? How can any one share with others this truth if the fire of the Spirit does not burn in him and purify him? A theologian who does not pray perseveringly, 'Grant to us, O Lord, a heart renewed' will gradually lose not only the sense of sin but also the sense of God. His vocation as a theologian is thoroughly linked to faith in his being called to holiness, together with all men.

Christian faith is not a system of abstract concepts, not a philosophy, and even less an ideology. The study and teaching of theology have to be understood as a saving event, an experience of God's creative, redeeming and sanctifying presence, and as a sign of the encounter with God that derives from his having called us. If the tools of theology fall into the hands of people who do not pray, then everything degenerates into ideologies and alienation. On the contrary, in the life of those theologians, teachers and students who not only pray but allow theology itself to be an act of openness to God's purifying presence and to the mission for the salvation of the world, alienation and blindness are gradually overcome.

Theology is faith searching for insight (*fides quaerens intellectum*) more than human insight searching for faith (*intellectus quaerens fidem*). For those who live an intensive life of prayer, theology is an act of faith that leads to an ever deepening knowledge of God and his saving design. This does not, however, exclude the other direction. Theology is also an ongoing effort to bring all human experiences and insights home to an integrated faith. Wisdom and intellect, gifts of the Holy Spirit, give to the theologian an increasing connaturality with the truth of faith. Since these are gifts of the Holy Spirit, they are granted only to those who pray and adore with all their heart.

Theology has its most vital centre in the Eucharist, where we learn to praise God for his gratuitous gifts. In this light and with this spirit, we also see human experience and competence as gifts of God, and they become, then, an integral part of the charism, of the special gifts of the Holy Spirit.

✛ We praise you, living Word of the Father, for those men and women to whom you have given the special charisma of theology. We thank you for theologians like St Paul and St John, whose whole reflection and message arose out of their life with you. The Church is suffering wherever pastors are neither theologians nor saints; and she suffers no less where theologians are neither pastoraly minded nor saints.

Grant to your Church, O Lord, that pastors, professional theologians and the faithful share together their faith, their insights and experiences, and thus grow in the knowledge of your name.

2. *Knowing God and knowing man*

Faith is an existential loving knowledge of God. God reveals himself, his love and, at the same time, his loving concern for man.

A living faith brings trustful and faithful adherence to God's self-revelation. 'This is eternal life: to know thee who alone are truly God, and him whom thou hast sent, Jesus Christ' (Jn 17:3). Christ is the way and the truth, who brings us to know the Father and to recognize the loftiness of our vocation as sons and daughters of the one God and Father.

In faith we know the most wonderful gifts of God, beyond the power of human reason to fathom: gifts which self-seeking men can never receive. 'At that moment Jesus rejoiced in the Holy Spirit and said, "I thank thee Father, Lord of heaven and earth, for what remains hidden from the wise and prudent, thou hast revealed to the simple. Yes, Father, such was thy choice". Then turning to his disciples he said, "Everything is entrusted to me by my Father; and no one knows who the Son is but the

Father, or who the Father is but the Son and those to whom
the Son may choose to reveal him" ' (Lk 10:21-22).

It is not God who conceals himself from the arrogant; it is
man's very arrogance that makes him unable to discover God's
self-revealing love. God wants to reveal himself to all people;
and therefore he gives us the grace to pray humbly and to
thank him for each new step in an ever-growing knowledge of
his love and his design.

For those who have no way of knowing Christ because he
is not rightly proclaimed to them, their neighbour can be the
image of God, to lead them to a vital knowledge of what is
good and right and just; and this can be a way of salvation.
Those who know Christ with a living faith are the chosen
instruments to make him known to others. As image and likeness of God, each of us becomes a very essential part of God's
revelation and so a motive of faith for all people, but especially
for those who know Jesus Christ.

For the theologian, a basic task is to work out a synthesis
between the knowledge of man derived from the revelation in
Christ, and that kind of knowledge which is the result of shared
experience and reflection. In this effort he cannot ignore the
behavioural sciences which help us to come to a more concrete
knowledge of the human person today.

The main purpose of theology is always to find a vital
synthesis between love of God and love of our neighbour, in
view of the present opportunities. Without a spirit of prayer,
this is impossible. A mere intellectual synthesis, severed from
experience of life and/or from adoration, can lead only to
illusions, abstractions, and alienation. Prayer, however, as Jesus
Christ taught it, as adoration of God in spirit and in truth,
is the heart both of theology and of an existential synthesis
between the knowledge and love of God and the knowledge
and love of man. We pray for the light and warmth that the
Holy Spirit gives, and that enable us to love man and the
world with the same love with which Christ, our Saviour, has
loved us.

A theology that is reduced to an intellectual technique or, even worse, to a battlefield of philosophical reasoning where antagonisms are bred against followers of other schools or trends of thought, is utterly lacking the heart and mind for the truth of salvation. It can provoke a sharp crisis of faith; and the theologian who indulges in this kind of 'theology' may have already lost faith without knowing it, while he is fighting fanatically for the most complete catalogue of formulations.

A theology that lacks an adoring awareness of God's presence is an embodiment of alienation and leads inevitably to a kind of orthodox heterodoxy, since those who do not entrust themselves humbly and gratefully to God will always make partial choices, emphasizing only those things that do not challenge their own ways. Such a theology can communicate a great many particular data but cannot lead to the kind of knowledge of God and man that brings salvation.

✛ O God, your love is so infinite that you want us to be sharers of it. You reveal yourself in all your works. I thank you for having revealed yourself to us in Jesus Christ and for continuing to reveal yourself more and more by sending us your Spirit.

Help us to share with each other your knowledge and your love, and thus grow in gratitude.

Lord, make us holy; Lord, make us humble, that we may know you ourselves and know our fellowmen with your own knowledge that breathes love.

3. How does theology become prayer?

Some people say, 'I don't need time for prayer; my whole life is prayer'; and some theologians may think, 'All my theology is prayer; I don't have to set time apart for prayer.'

It is true that, according to God's design, all theology and all Christian life is prayer. However, in the hands of us sinners, the ideal seldom becomes the reality. We all have to strive constantly to be true Christians, and equally, the theologian has to strive unceasingly to make his theology a truthful adoration of God.

We should all think with St Paul, 'It is not to be thought that I have already achieved all this. I have not yet reached perfection but I press on, hoping to take hold of that for which Christ once took hold of me. My friends, I do not reckon myself to have got hold of it yet. All I can say is this: forgetting what is behind me, I reach out for that which lies ahead' (Phil 3:12-14). We need to help each other in this endeavour, and while we do so, we become more fully aware of our need of God's help for our on-going conversion. Faith lives and becomes more vital in the community of believers that helps us to grow in the spirit of prayer.

The community of theologians, teachers and students, all disciples of Christ, should constitute an exemplary community of faith. To study theology together means to be gathered around Christ, our Master, who makes us friends and brothers to each other.

It is a great gain that in most of the theological faculties and seminaries now, professors and students frequently concelebrate the Eucharist. Also, in various places I have seen and assisted at communal celebrations of reconciliation with a shared examination of conscience and shared prayer of thanksgiving and praise for God's mercy. It is a hopeful sign, too, that in many places students and professors come together, outside of lecture time, for shared prayer. They listen together to the word of God without the technicality of a theological lecture. They meditate on it and, as the Spirit inspires them, they share their insights and their sentiments of praise, gratitude and mutual encouragement. Such a community will learn the prayer of vigilance: how to respond to God's word in our daily life.

But it is surely not sufficient to promote shared prayer outside of and besides actual theological study. Theology itself must, more and more, take on the form of adoration and fraternal love in the love of the Lord. The personal study of theology and the theological lecture should increase loving adoration of God as much as knowledge of God, and at the same time enkindle an active and enlightened love of our neighbour.

With this goal, each theological lecture should begin with prayer, though normally not with a recitation of prayers but with a prayer that anticipates in some way the main theme of the lecture. The spontaneous prayer often helps us to become aware of God's presence better than does the daily recitation of the same prayer. The lecture should then conclude with another prayer of praise and thanksgiving about the truths which were communicated and reflected on together. It is not necessary that the professor always say this prayer; rather, it is closer to the ideal if students themselves take the opportunity to share this concluding prayer with the others.

Unforgettable for many of us is a lecture by Karl Adam on Christology. At a certain point he had to interrupt the lecture because he was so deeply moved that he could not utter any words. This silence was more eloquent than many other lectures by professors who never gave witness of their personal faith and of love for Christ.

If we speak of prayer and theology, then pastoral concern can never be left out, because theology is a service of love and salvation. It is not possible to grow in the knowledge of man without experiencing an ever-growing zeal for his salvation. A theology is truly alive only in so far as it finds a synthesis between prayer and a pastoral spirit, between worship and apostolate. The contribution that each theologian, teacher or student, can give to this synthesis is in direct proportion to the integration between faith and life that he has reached in his own life. A prayerful theology will always make us sensitive to the groaning of the whole created universe which longs to have a share in the liberty and the splendour of the children of God (Rom 8:21-23).

✝ We pray you, Almighty Father, to grant to your Church theologians who are humble disciples of your Servant, Jesus Christ, and whose first concern is 'Lord, teach us how to pray.'

We thank you for all the saints who were theologians and for all the theologians who were at the same time saints. We thank you for all the pastors whose concern is to grow in the knowledge of you and of mankind, and to teach their people how to pray.

Help us to contemplate the mysteries of the Word Incarnate, so that our life and our words can communicate the harvest of the Spirit: love, joy, peace, benevolence.

Inspire in us an ardent desire to love and to know you and your Son, Jesus Christ, more and more intimately.

And grant us that joy of faith which is the very heart of theology and of the gladdening news.

Chapter 4

THE PRAYER OF VIGILANCE

There are people who seek transcendental meditation, contemplation, prayer, because they are dissatisfied with life. They are seeking God beyond and outside of history. An authentic Christian concept of prayer does not allow this kind of evasion; prayer is not flight from history and everyday reality. Surely God is infinitely greater than the world around us, but if we find him and centre our attention and love on him, then he opens our eyes and our minds, and we see more in life than the distracted or self-centred person can ever envisage.

Christian prayer is an expression of vigilance for God's coming into our human history. The Lord teaches us at the same time prayer and vigilance. 'Be on the alert and pray at all times for strength' (Lk 21:36). Especially in all decisive moments we must pray; but we cannot pray if we are not willing to be alert and ready for the coming of the Lord in the hour of decision. But neither can we be truly ready to receive him in the decisive moments without a spirit of prayer.

1. *The history of salvation as the coming of the Lord*

The last chapter of the gospel of St John tells of an event that is not easily understood. When Peter was forgiven and reconfirmed in his ministry, he turned and saw John, the beloved disciple. Peter knew well that John had been far more faithful to the Lord than he himself had been, and would deserve the first place. So he asked the Lord, 'Lord, what will happen to him?' In response, Jesus pointed to John's great charisma. 'So if it is my wish that he be a man waiting for my coming, what does this mean to you?' (Jn 21:21-22).

Many disciples misunderstood this. They thought that Jesus was indicating that John was not to die but would live until his final coming at the parousia. The gospel insists, however, that this was not Jesus' message to Peter: that what he said was something much more important for the life of the Church.

Not only Peter but the whole Church, office-holders and people, have to ask themselves about the profound meaning of John's charism. He represents those believers who, through a great love for the Lord and a deep understanding of history, are always ready to greet the Lord when he comes, in whatever disguise he may appear.

Christian prayer inserts the believer wholly into the history of salvation. Faith means to live in the presence of the One who was, who comes and who will come. To live in the presence of the Lord of history means to be alive to the grace of the present moment. The alienated person, who is today everywhere in the secular city and unfortunately exists also in religious bodies, indulges in wishful thoughts: 'if only ... if only ...'.
But one who believes in the Lord of history faces reality here and now and discovers its hidden treasures.

John, the beloved disciple, is always the first to recognize the Lord, whether he comes during the dark night or in disguise, as at Lake Tiberius. The symbol of the fourth evangelist is the eagle: he has the eagle's eye. Because of his great love, he knows the Master even when he comes as a surprise. A humble and grateful faith, a profound love of the Master, does not try to impose one's own desires and plans on God, but adores him even when his coming is unexpected and somehow painful.

One of the great themes of St John's first letter is the surprising coming of the Lord in our neighbour. In those who need our love, as well as in those who manifest a Christlike love, Christ does meet us and test us. One cannot love the invisible God if one does not welcome his visible image. God the Father comes into our lives through Jesus Christ, but also through the poor, the handicapped, the psychopath who needs our respect, our love, our help.

Those who have the charisma of the beloved disciple, who are persons authentically waiting for the Lord's coming, have a profound vision of human history. They see all events in the light of Christ's first coming into our human situation as brother among brethren, as servant of God and man. Thanksgiving for this first coming of the Lord turns their eyes and hearts towards his final coming in glory. Between these two forms of his coming is the present moment with its grace and its challenge.

Whoever is grateful for the coming of the Lord as servant of all, will use fully the present opportunities. In the name of Christ, his vigilant disciples will show mercy to those who are in need, respect to those who are degraded, love to those whom nobody wants to love. They will greet them as beloved brothers and sisters, because it is the hour of Christ's own coming. Thus they can look forward with joy to the final coming of the Lord at the end of human history.

The gospel tells us consistently that the Lord will come at an hour and in a manner beyond all human expectations and calculations. Vigilance is that virtue that adores God and allows him, as Lord, full freedom to call us in whatever way he likes. When God truly comes into our life, there is always a strong element of surprise that challenges us and imposes on us a revision of our desires and programmes. For the sleepy, the superficial and the arrogant, this coming can be a sudden and disturbing awakening. But for the disciples of Christ, the prayer of vigilance, the adoration that becomes readiness, has prepared them for his coming even when it seems to be the greatest surprise. In their prayer they have learned that the Lord is always infinitely greater than we are, and he manifests his greatest love when he offers us what we did not pray for and calls us for what we did not want to do.

✝   Here I am, Lord; you have come into my life from the very beginning.

You have given me a body and life.

You have made me what I am: here I am, O Lord, to do your will.

Here I am, O Lord; send me wherever you want.

Make me ready, keep me awake, cleanse my heart even with fire, even by cross and suffering, by difficulties and opposition.

Lord, take away from me everything that hinders me from recognizing your coming.

Lord, grant everything that leads me closer to you.

Lord, here I am; call me; send me.

2. *Sleeper, awake*

In the New Testament, the call to conversion for Christians who had become superficial and lazy was, 'Sleeper, awake, and let Christ shine upon you' (Eph 5:16). Christ distinguishes between sleepy and vigilant virgins.

Vigilance is a gift of the Holy Spirit. It is an open mind, an attentive ear, a sensitivity to the needs of others and a readiness to serve. It is a life characterized by listening and responding to the Lord.

The vigilant person will surely take enough hours to sleep, to relax; there will be no lack of a sense of humour; and yet there will be an alertness and readiness like that of a mother who, in the midst of her activity, hears her child the moment he needs her. Vigilance means a life that, on all practical occasions, spells out the prayer to our Father, 'Thy will be done on earth as it is in heaven.'

Because he always lives in the light of Christ, the vigilant Christian perceives the grace of each hour, of each time of decision, as a call coming from the Lord. He treasures the gospel in his heart and ponders over it. His life in the presence of the Lord makes him value each moment with its limited and yet sometimes great possibilities to respond to the Lord's presence.

Vigilance and discernment go hand in hand. Both are gifts of the Spirit. After the call, 'Sleeper, awake', the apostle of the Gentiles exhorts Christians, 'Be most careful, then, how you conduct yourselves: like sensible men, not like simpletons. Use the present opportunities to the full, for these are evil days. So do not be fools, but try to understand what the will of the Lord is. Do not give way to drunkenness and dissipation but let the Holy Spirit fill you' (Eph 5:15-18).

The prayer of vigilance is a personal and often a shared meditation on life's conditions, in an effort to discern what the true countenance of love is, and what would be a fitting response to God in the concrete situation in which he calls us. When St Paul insists that we 'use the present opportunities to the full', his Greek verb brings to mind the alert steward or the wise housewife who knows when and how to make the best purchases.

In Greek, the right moment is called *kairos*. It is not the time that ticks away always at the same speed, but the given moment with its offer of opportunities. This and the other Greek word *hora* are key words in the New Testament. Christ repeatedly speaks of his hour, 'the hour prepared by the Father'. He himself stands before us as incarnate readiness for that hour.

The Bible sometimes speaks even of 'the *kairos* of temptation'. The most tempting situation can become, for those who live habitually in the light of the Lord, a call to holiness, to a firm and total decision. It can become the moment of a creative leap forward.

One who prays with all his heart, mind and will, comes to accept himself and others, and the concrete situations of his life. The first necessity is surely to accept oneself with a realistic faith, with one's own good qualities and one's shadows, though sometimes with a painful awareness of limitations. Why should we waste time and energy in evasive thoughts, in longing for qualities or conditions that we do not have? The person who knows how to pray, and thus to become alert for the coming of the Lord in his own situation, accepts even his own failures. They can help him become more humble, more understanding of others, and allow him to discover his true capacities to serve God and his fellowmen.

The prayer of vigilance makes us sensitive to sins of omission. Those who do not live in the presence of the Lord of history are always tempted to consider only the general rules and principles, and to overlook the concrete opportunities. But those whose thinking is shaped by the Eucharist will render thanks always and everywhere, and thus be ready to recognize and to use the gifts offered them in the actual circumstances of their life. They will be appreciative of the goodness of their fellow-men and alert to their needs. Their examination of conscience will concentrate not only on the decalogue, or even on the more demanding and pressing affirmatives of the New Testament, but even more on the grace, the talents received, and the real possibilities which they may have neglected throughout the days.

Such an examination of conscience and act of sorrow will be a constant reminder, 'Sleeper, awake, and let Christ shine upon you'. Our act of sorrow will then not be worrying but will express trust in the Lord who calls us again. Sorrow and purpose become a renewed readiness to greet the Lord when he comes, when he calls us through his gifts and our neighbour's needs. We shall then be one with our brothers and sisters in their joys and sorrows, their anguish and their hopes, and can become for them a sign of hope, an effective sign of the Lord's gracious presence.

Repeatedly we have meditated on the relation between

thanksgiving and hope, both of which call us to be alert and ready for the grace of the present moment. The more we are sensitive to all that God has already done for us and for mankind, and the more we look forward to the blessed coming of the Lord at the end of history and the end of our life, the more we shall appreciate the given hour. Indeed, awareness of present opportunities is the most intensive act of thanksgiving and of hope. We live in the presence of the Lord by fully accepting and using this moment as the concrete possibility to render thanks to him and to entrust ourselves to him. At the same time, we give thanks also for all those people who have prepared for us this time of opportunity. And we exercise responsibility for the future not only for ourselves but also for the benefit of our fellowmen. We cannot render thanks to the Lord who was, who is, and who will come, without being alert and ready for his coming in the here and now.

✠ I thank you, O Lord, for calling me to your presence by making me alert to the opportunities that are opened to me day by day.

It is always you, our Lord of history, who give true dimensions and open new horizons to our limited and fleeting moments.

Whatever comes into my life calls me to you and thus helps me to find my own name.

Lord, make me more alert for your coming. Let me be a sharer of your own creativity and thus able to redeem, for myself and for others, each hour of decision which you prepare for me.

3. Fidelity and readiness to change

The prayer of vigilance means living the grace of each hour with intense gratitude and hope. It is an ever-renewed, 'Yes, Lord, here I am to do your will', and the ever new experience of God's coming into our life, of his being with us on our way. This gives to our life continuity and, at the same time, the willingness to change. It is the continuity of those who walk in the presence of the Lord; it is an ongoing conversion, in constant readiness to explore new ways and to walk ever more energetically with the Lord.

God does not change his design; he is always infinite love and fidelity. But he is not immobile. He is the Lord of history, who comes to meet us in new and surprising ways. We human beings are sinning both by immobility — the unwillingness to make necessary changes — and by infidelity to our best intentions. Our clinging to past forms of life once seemed to give us security but is now usually no more than a security complex. Our selfishness, and often the narrowness of our environment, also block our road and limit our life's horizons. In a truthful life of prayer, our eyes and minds open to new horizons that grow constantly wider and more attractive. Gradually we free ourselves from our timidity, our superficiality, self-centredness and narrowness, and place our trust in the Lord. We are on the road with him.

The prayer of vigilance is the willingness to live personally the exodus of the people of God and of Christ himself. When God called Abraham to walk before him, he also invited him to leave his homeland. Moses was the man of God who experienced with unique intensity the presence of God, but then all his life became an exodus. We live today in an historical moment that is itself a gigantic exodus. The younger generation lives a new culture; traditional values are being questioned, negated or transposed; the centres of influence are moving towards the third world. We can carry out our mission as Christians only if we are ready to act and give witness in this new kind of world.

In such an age, the prayer of vigilance gives us trust in the Lord of history. Those who entrust themselves to God in readiness to live the great exodus required by the present history of salvation, find their sabbath, their peace, in the real continuity

of life. Our Lord is always the same; his design is abiding love
and peace. He is the faithful one under whatever guise he meets
us. His coming is, as it has always been, a call to a more
intimate friendship and to the honoured task of being co-
creators and co-revealers of his love in this time and age.

Again it becomes clear that Christian prayer cannot be a
mere repetition or recitation of formulas. Certainly the beautiful
prayers of saints of all ages are not to be undervalued; they
are for us a school where we may learn to pray and to be
vigilant. The condition for learning from them and making good
use of them, however, is that we are ready to live according
to the grace of the hour that is now given to us. Thus our own
prayer can never be a stereotyped repetition of the prayers of
the past. By meditating on them we learn to pay attention to
the signs of the present times and to discover what the creative
and generous response to our vocation and mission should be
in the new circumstances of life. Always, in one way or another,
our prayer will express, 'Lord, here I am; call me, send me'.

The Christian knows that all authentic contemplative prayer
is in the Word Incarnate. His attitude therefore to contemplation is very different from the concept of neo-platonism or
Buddhism. His communion through Christ in the inner life of
the Godhead is an encounter also with the Lord of history in
his coming here and now, in view of his final coming. We can,
of course, learn much from the great intellectual and religious
traditions that have found ways to free men's minds from
distraction and tension and have learned how to explore the
inner space; but Christian prayer and contemplation include
an element of mission and a dimension of which even the best
non-Christian contemplatives seem unconscious. If we seek
peace and repose before the Lord, we do it also in view of our
mission to be messengers of peace and reconciliation in the
world.

In the prayer of vigilance there is an element of wholesome
disquiet. Attention to the Lord's coming does disturb the old
Adam or old Eve in us. It does upset security complexes and

overthrow the traditionalist in us. To believe in God's kingdom
with one's whole heart and mind is an awakening to alertness
and readiness. Anyone who, in his prayer, declares himself ready
for the Lord's calling will find it reasonable that God disturbs
our circles and overthrows our human planning wherever he
wants. If, in our prayer, we stand before the Lord of history,
we become sensitive to the promptings of the Spirit and gradually realize the blessing of the exodus to which God calls
everyone and every group. It is an exodus from the selfish self
to the true self that is ready to serve God through our brethren.

The prophets are models of the prayer of vigilance. The
Spirit of the Lord made them ready to unmask injustice, to
decry false peace and pious lies. The prayer of vigilance dis-
poses us to believe in the Holy Spirit who speaks through the
prophets and makes us aware that we too, from time to time,
are pious liars.

In the vigilant prayer of his disciples, Christ continues his
own prayer. 'At his coming into the world he says: sacrifice
and ritual offering thou didst not desire, but thou hast prepared
a body for me. Therefore I said, "Here I am: as it is written
of me in the scrolls, I have come, O God, to do thy will" '
(Heb 10:5-7). Jesus, who was always vigilant and ready for
the hour prepared by the Father, accomplishes all his work in
the final prayer, 'Father, into thy hands I commit my spirit'
(Lk 23:46). From this prayer of the Lord, in the midst of his
suffering, all our prayer draws its strength.

✛ Lord, you are always with us; you come constantly into
our lives; you wait for our coming to you.

From you I receive, each day anew, my name, my life,
my capacity to love my brothers and sisters, all those who love
me or allow me to love them.

All and everything is your gift, a message of your love, a
sign of your coming.

Lord, you are always with us; you call us and wait always
for us.

Make us grateful; make us vigilant.

In all our joys, in the light of the sun, in the immensity of the firmament, in a child's smile, a mother's kindness, a father's strength, it is always you who come to meet us and to call us.

Lord, you are always with us; you call us and wait for us. Make us grateful and vigilant.

Lord, you have promised us wonderful things: that we shall always be with you. All that you have done and entrusted to us is a part of your promise, a sign of your faithfulness.

You have promised us the beatitude of a life where you are, with all our brethren, all your children.

Now, in this time in-between, you are our Way. You are on the road with us, the road that leads to you and the final joy of your presence.

Lord, you are always near to us; you call us and wait for us. Make us grateful; make us ready.

Each day is a new revelation of your love.

You multiply the signs of your kindness and goodness.

Each day you give us the strength to listen to you, to become more aware of your presence and to respond to you.

You have given us ears to hear when you call us through your Word and through our brothers and sisters.

Each day you open our eyes to see and to admire your works.

Each day you allow us to discover the signs of your coming, where others hear only noise and see only disaster.

Lord, you are always near to us; you come each day to call us.

You always wait for us.

Make us grateful, make us vigilant.

Lord, you are the great artist.

Day by day you carry on your work to make man as your masterpiece, the image of your own goodness and kindness.

It is for this that you send us rain as well as sunshine, suffering as well as pure joy.

So you call each of us by a unique name.

Your love for me is always love for my neighbour too.

Grant that, for all my brothers and sisters, I may be a sign of your coming, of your being with us and accomplishing your work of transforming us into signs of your goodness, of your presence.

Lord, you are always near to us; you always call us, always wait for us. Make us grateful and vigilant.

Lord, you have given us our parents to reveal to us your kindness and your tender love.

Each day you send us friends who, by their gentleness, draw our attention to you.

You send us people who are so generous that only you can be the source and the fulfilment of their good will.

You allow us to meet people who receive us and encourage us, and so help us to experience your love, that gives us the greatest hope.

You send us people who listen to us and understand us. Then we know again that you always listen to us and understand us.

Lord, you are always with us; you call us and wait for us.

Make us grateful, Lord; make us alert.

Then, O Lord, you lead us to those who are in sorrow and in need of comfort.

You come in the guise of the poor and allow us to make them rich with your goodness.

You bring to us those who are disillusioned and discouraged, so that we may be a sign of your consolation and encouragement.

You send us, O Lord, at the same time, so many gifts of your goodness, and those who are in need of love, so that we may transform your love into love for our brethren and thus, all together, we can experience that you are always with us, that you call us and wait for us.

Lord, make us vigilant and generous.

All our life waits for your final coming.

With complete trust I look forward to the hour of your call through my brother, Death. You yourself will come to meet me, to call me by my own name, the name you have given me. Then I shall know that your judgement is salvation and compassion if I now faithfully respond to your coming whenever and wherever you call me through my brother, the poor.

Come, Lord, call me whenever you want, under whatever conditions you decide. Only let me experience that it is your coming, your calling me.

Abide with us, O Lord. Maranatha; come, Lord Jesus. Make us vigilant and ready for your coming.

Chapter 5

THE PRAYER OF FAITH

The Creed is prayer. It is a grateful response to God's self-revelation. It should bring a constant growth in the knowledge of God and in our commitment to his saving plan.

Since the main concern of all these meditations is *integration of faith and life,* I offer here a few examples of how, within the liturgy, or in prayer groups and in our private meditations, we can treasure up the truth of faith in our hearts in view of the most urgent values of our time.

1. *Faith in man's dignity*

✛ Lord God, we believe that you, the almighty Father, have created men and women in your image and likeness. We believe, therefore, in the dignity of every human being as your son or daughter. But Father, we are weak and self-centred. Our faith will be truthful and this profession of our faith will honour you only when we truly honour every person and help each other, in mutual love and respect, to become more fully your likeness.

Lord, we believe; help us where our faith is falling short.

We believe in your Son, the one Lord, Jesus Christ, the almighty Word in whom you have made all things. In him

114

you speak all your love to the world. In obedience to your will, he chose to be our brother and thus to reveal that you are the one Father of all. His love for those who were the most despised has given us hope for a new creation. Through our faith in him, let us discover more and more the dignity of our brothers and sisters, even the most degraded or despised.

Lord, we believe; help us where our faith is falling short.

We believe that your only begotten Son came down from heaven for us and for our salvation, to free us from the slavery of sin and thus restore our dignity and make us worthy of you, Father. Help us to discover and revere, in ourselves and in all our fellowmen, Christ who brings us to wholeness if we share in his mission of saving love for all people. Then our faith will be a source of joy and dignity for us all.

Lord, we believe; help us where our faith is falling short.

We believe that Jesus, your Son, became man not to be served but to serve: to break the fetters of greed and the lust for power that have degraded your people, the exploiters and exploited alike. Father, give us the courage to follow your Son, to dedicate ourselves to his work of redemption by helping each other to find the meaning, wholeness and dignity for which you created us. Then our faith will be sincere.

Lord, we believe; help us where our faith is falling short.

We believe that your Son, Jesus Christ, was crucified, died and was buried. He was crucified not by the rabble but by people like us: men who had been taught by the prophets and who professed justice. Yet he prayed for them, his enemies, and made a friend of the criminal who, as further insult, was crucified beside him. Thus he transformed all the humiliation into a revelation of his own supreme dignity as your Son, and the renewed dignity of all your people.

Lord, we believe; help us where our faith is falling short.

We believe that your Son will come again to judge the

living and the dead, and that those who have honoured the
weak, the oppressed and the exploited will stand at his right
hand and be honoured as his brothers and sisters, your sons
and daughters.

Lord, we believe; help us where our faith is falling short.

We believe in the Holy Spirit, the Lord and giver of life.
With you, the Father, and your Son, he is worshipped and
glorified. His gifts call us to honour our own dignity and that
of our fellowmen. He gives us the power to create a divine
milieu in which everyone can find his place and realize his
worthiness; thus he renews the face of the earth and the hearts
of men.

Lord, we believe; help us where our faith is falling short.

We believe, Father, in one holy, catholic and apostolic
Church. Help us, Father, to be truthful to this one faith by
honouring each other — especially the weakest among us — as
members of the one body of Christ. We attest to our faith in
this Church wherever we promote peace, social justice and
respect for the dignity of every person, since we are all created
by you, the Father of all.

Lord, we believe; help us where our faith is falling short.

We acknowledge one baptism for the forgiveness of sins.
We praise you, Father, for the baptism of your Son, Jesus
Christ, during a general baptism in the Jordan. By his presence
with those who knew they were sinners, he restored the dignity
of all of us sinners. We praise you, too, for the baptism of your
Son in his own blood as a sign of his solidarity with all humankind. And we praise you for his baptism by the Holy Spirit.
Baptized by the same Spirit, we can recognize in ourselves and
in our fellowmen the dignity of the new creation.

Lord, we believe; help us where our faith is falling short.

We look forward to the resurrection of the dead and the
life in the communion of saints. This faith and this hope,

Father, can be no illusion for us when we are restored by the power of your Holy Spirit, and do all in our power to honour the dignity of all people and to create, here on earth, an environment in which each person can live an honoured life.

Lord, we believe; help us where our faith is falling short.

2. Faith in joy

We believe in one God, the Father of all mankind.

To know that you, the Creator of all things, are our almighty Father is our greatest joy. Father, make us worthy children. If we truly believe in you, our weakness and our deficiencies cannot rob us of this joy.

Lord, we believe; grant us a joyous faith.

We believe in one Lord, Jesus Christ, the only Son of God, eternally begotten of the Father.

Father, you have spoken all your love and all your beatitude in your only Son. All that you have created in him, the almighty Word, is a message of joy, a promise of beatitude.

Lord we believe; grant us a joyous faith.

For us men and for our salvation he came down from heaven. By the power of the Holy Spirit he was born of the virgin Mary and became man.

We praise you, Father, for having revealed yourself as our Father by sending us your only begotten Son as our brother, our friend, our saviour.

Lord, we believe; grant us a joyous faith.

For our sake he was crucified under Pontius Pilate; he suffered, died and was buried. On the third day he rose again in fulfilment of the scriptures.

Suffering, sin and the fear of death, O Lord Jesus, often prevent people from rejoicing in you; but if we truly believe in you, we are free from the slavery of sin and the fear of death. Then even suffering has a new meaning. Your suffering, your passion and death are the manifestation of your infinite love for us. Therefore, in gratitude and trust we can join you, bearing our cross day by day and sharing one another's burdens. This is the road of your beatitudes.

Lord, we believe. Lord, grant us a joyous faith.

He ascended into heaven and is seated at the right hand of the Father. His kingdom will have no end.

Lord, we rejoice in the victory of your love; we rejoice in your glory. And even in the midst of the storms of this life, we know that we can entrust ourselves to you. To serve you is to share in your kingdom.

Lord, we believe; grant us a joyous faith.

We believe in the Holy Spirit, the Lord, the giver of life.

Come, Holy Spirit; help us to treasure up the word of Christ in our hearts, to see in all events and in all the works of the Father his message of joy, his call to live according to the beatitudes. If we are docile to you, our lives will bear fruit in joy, in kindness, in gentleness.

Lord, we believe; grant us a joyous faith.

We believe in one holy, catholic, apostolic Church.

Your Church, Lord, is a community of faith. She proclaims to us the gospel and teaches us the morality of the gospel: that you are the Way, the Truth, the Life. To be united in one faith is a source of unending joy.

Lord, we believe; we rejoice in our faith. Grant us a joyous faith.

We acknowledge one baptism for the forgiveness of sins.

What would our life be, Almighty Father, if we had not come to know that your Son, Jesus Christ, was baptized for us in water, in blood and in the Spirit, to free us from our guilt, to forgive us and reconcile us. Help us to fulfil the law of Christ by helping each other, correcting and encouraging each other, and bearing one another's burdens. Then sin can never overcome us.

Lord, we believe; grant us a joyous faith.

We look forward to the resurrection of the dead and the life of the world to come.

Lord, we are saved in hope because you are faithful. You never abandon those who put their faith and hope in you; and this hope is the joy of our life.

Lord, we believe; grant us always a joyous faith.

3. Faith in unity and solidarity

We believe in one God, the almighty Father.

Only you, almighty Father, can gather your people and bring them together in mutual respect and generous concern for one another. Created in your image and likeness, we can have a share in the almighty power of your love, and become one, if we truly believe in you and put our trust in you.

Lord, we believe. Lord, make us holy; make us one.

We believe in Jesus Christ, the only Son of the Father: light from light, true God from true God. Through him all things were made.

Lord Jesus Christ, you are one with the Father. You are the living Word in whom all things are made. You call together all people, and appeal to us to see everything as your gift for all and to use all your gifts in solidarity and for unity.

Lord, we believe. Lord, make us holy; make us one.

For us men and for our salvation he came down from heaven; by the power of the Holy Spirit he was born of the virgin Mary and became man.

Jesus, Son of the living God, son of David, son of Mary,

we believe that you can gather your people together and bring us to holiness. For you have come to reconcile us with our Father and to reconcile us with each other.

Lord, we believe. Lord, make us holy; make us one.

For our sake he was crucified under Pontius Pilate; he suffered, died and was buried. On the third day he rose again in fulfilment of the scriptures. He ascended into heaven and is seated at the right hand of the Father.

Jesus Christ, our Saviour, all this you have done for us, to make us the people of the covenant. How can we, then, endure hatred and enmity, divisions and jealousies among ourselves? If we firmly believe in you and put our trust in you, we can put to death our selfish concerns and become a new creation, one with you and one with each other.

Lord we believe. Lord, make us holy; make us one.

He will come again in glory to judge the living and the dead, and his kingdom will have no end.

We believe in your kingdom, Lord. Even now we can have a share in it if we are one: if we make peace with each other, if we are one with the poor, one with the lowly and lonely, one with those who are angry and frustrated. We can look forward to your coming in glory when we have fed the hungry, have visited the sick and have freed the captives.

Lord, we believe. Lord, make us holy; make us one.

We believe in the Holy Spirit, the Lord, the giver of life, who proceeds from the Father and the Son. With the Father and the Son he is worshipped and glorified.

Come, Holy Spirit, help us to share your gifts generously with each other, and to accept one another in spite of our differences in temperament, opinions and preferences. Lead us, through your gifts and the needs of our fellowmen, to unite in a sincere search for unity, peace and reconciliation among all people.

Lord, we believe. Lord, make us holy; make us one.

We believe in one holy, catholic and apostolic Church.

Faith in you, Lord, brings us eternal life, if we live our vocation to holiness by being truly one with all your people. Help us to witness to the oneness, the holiness, the universality, and the apostolic character of your Church by serving the unity of all mankind, all social classes and all nations, in mutual respect and solidarity.

Lord, we believe. Lord, make us holy; make us one. *Amen*

We look forward to the resurrection of the dead and the life of the world to come.

Lord, in the new heaven and on the new earth, there will be no divisions, no isolation, no egotism. Our faith and our hope in you set us on the right path, on the way to unity, and make us ready to live according to this hope and this faith.

Lord, we believe. Lord, make us holy; make us one.

4. *Faith in freedom and commitment to liberation*

We believe in one God, the almighty Father. He has made us to be his free sons and daughters. He alone can free us, through his almighty love, from the slavery of sin, self-destruction and mutual oppression. He wants us to love him and each other with a generosity born of freedom.

Lord, we believe in your almighty love. Lord, make us free.

We believe that all things visible and invisible have been made by the almighty Father for all his people to share in freedom and to use for their unity in freedom.

Lord, free us from individual and group selfishness, exploitation and oppression. Lord, we believe. Lord, make us free.

We believe that Jesus Christ, the Son of the almighty Father, came, in his own freedom, to carry out his Father's design to liberate mankind from oppression and domination.

Lord God, we believe in the freedom of your Son, your Servant. We believe that he alone can lead us on the way to liberty. Lord, we believe. Lord, make us free.

We believe that the Son of God made himself poor to make us rich. In obedience to his Father's will to reveal to us his liberating love, he freely accepted death on the cross; but by his resurrection, he won the victory of full liberation.

Lord, if we truly believe, we shall follow you on the way to liberty. Lord, we believe. Lord, make us free.

We believe in the Holy Spirit, giver of all good gifts and source of freedom in brotherhood. We believe that those who truly pray and cry out in the Spirit, 'Our Father!', will be sensitive to the longing of all creation for a share in the liberty of the sons and daughters of God. And we believe that those who accept the gifts of the Spirit as their programme of life will be free to create a world in which true liberty has a dwelling place.

Lord, we do believe. Lord, make us free.

We believe that the Holy Spirit has spoken through the prophets and still sends us prophets to challenge the oppressors and exploiters of their fellowmen. We truly believe in the Spirit if we humbly listen to the voices of the prophets and the voice of Christ the Prophet, who came to release the prisoners, to make us all free brothers and sisters, and channels of his peace.

Lord, we believe. Lord, make us free.

We believe in the holy, catholic and apostolic Church, called to be a great sacrament of liberty and liberation. We believe in her mission, and honour her when we unite in the commitment to free mankind from the age-old slavery of war, violence, oppression and exploitation, and accept our mission as ambassadors of reconciliation.

Lord, we believe. Lord, make us free and send us as messengers of peace and freedom.

We believe in one baptism for the forgiveness of sins. We believe that Christ came to baptize us with the Holy Spirit and to make us free sons and daughters of the Father, free from selfishness and group egotism. We believe in Christ's own baptism in water, in his blood and in the Spirit. And we believe that we can live our own baptism only by accepting our mission to be co-revealers of Christ's love for the world and co-workers with him in the history of liberation.

Lord, help us to respect the freedom of our fellowmen and to work together for the freedom of all people and all nations. Lord, we believe. Lord, make us free.

We believe in the communion of the saints, in the resurrection of the body and in life everlasting. We believe that we can look forward in hope and trust to the moment when we shall be freed from the shackles of corruption and death, if we live now the joyful liberty of the sons and daughters of God and commit ourselves to transforming the world around us by the liberating power of brotherhood and justice.

Lord, we believe. Lord, make us free.

Chapter 6

SHARED PRAYER

1. *Religious experience and shared prayer*

In the wake of anti-modernism, the phrase 'religious experience' practically disappeared from the Catholic vocabulary. Instead, 'objective prayer' was emphasized. Each prayer composed for recitation in public had first to be submitted to the ecclesiastical authorities; and what they were looking for was not whether it was the most vital experience of personal and communal faith but whether the formula was dogmatically correct.

However, in the mainstream of Catholic tradition — indeed in all Christian churches — there has always been a high appreciation of religious experience. The Old Testament concept of 'the glory of God' is generally linked to a deep experience of God's holiness and to overwhelming joy in the experience of God's presence. In the communities of St Teresa of Avila and of St John of the Cross, religious experience played a very substantial role.

The first vigorous reaction against the anti-modernist fear of religious experience was the youth movement in Germany and France between the First and Second World Wars. Now, in North America and in almost all parts of the world, young

124

people are looking again for authentic religious experience. They express their faith in an immediate and spontaneous way, and share it not only as a profession of faith but also as an expression of the solidarity of salvation.

With the Second Vatican Council's renewed emphasis on the presence of the Holy Spirit among believers, it was inevitable that the Church would again give a place to spontaneity and creativity in communal as well as in personal prayer. 'All who are led by the Spirit of God are sons of God. You did not receive a spirit of slavery so as to be again in fear, but a spirit of adoption through which we cry out, "Abba! Father!". The Spirit within us gives witness with our spirit that we are children of God' (Rom 8:14-16).

Spontaneous shared prayer is like a choir in which the various voices profess the one faith in the one Father, the one hope in the one Redeemer, Jesus Christ, and trust in the one Spirit. Sometimes, in gatherings of pentecostals or charismatic renewal groups, we can hear that they sing in tongues, and even though they have not previously practised, all the voices join in one great harmony. This is a symbol of what shared prayer is in its deepest theological meaning.

Shared prayer has great relevance for the Church in these times of rapid cultural transformation. It manifests that we are living with the God of history. We are moved by the Spirit and we express our faith as people of this time and age. God is not dead. In both personal and communal expression, spontaneous prayer not only helps to overcome the crisis of faith but has also a real impact on the evangelization of the world of today. It will also help to prepare the Church for a more lively liturgical worship.

I know a group of missionaries in Africa who are regularly invited into numerous Mohammedan villages to meditate with the inhabitants. They read a part of the Koran and, even more often, the parables of the gospel. All participate with great enthusiasm, expressing their thoughts and feelings, and praising

the Lord together. It is a meeting of shared prayer and, indeed,
a wonderful sharing of their faith in the one God and Father
of all, as well as a way of honouring Jesus Christ, the only
perfect monotheist and the Prophet. I am convinced that the
evangelization of today's world depends greatly on this kind of
religious experience.

2. What is shared prayer?

It has always been recognized that a community of faith is
unthinkable without a coming together for prayer and adoration
of the one God and Father. What I am insisting on here is the
spontaneity with which faith, hope and love are shared in
meetings for prayer today.

At least in the present situation, it is not normal for people
to come together only to recite preformulated prayers without
allowing themselves any spontaneity and creativity. The prayer
I speak of, which is found at the present time in almost all
parts of Christianity and especially in the Catholic Church, is
a very particular openness of spirit and mutual trust by those
who share their insights, their experiences, their purpose, joy
and concern in a very simple way. Just as adult sons or daughters
would never confine their dialogue with their parents to the
recitation of poetry or to readings from the classics, so we, when
we come together to pray, want to act as the family of God and
respond to the grace of the present hour.

There are as many models of these meetings for prayer as
there are cultures and people. I will try to explain briefly one
model that is used very often. It is the shared prayer of the
Quakers. The same kind has a long tradition in the Catholic
Church. It was propagated more than two centuries ago by
St Alphonsus of Liguori, the great moralist and teacher of
prayer. As a young priest he founded many prayer groups in
and around Naples. The model is very simple.

The group, when it has gathered, is led into prayer either

by a traditional prayer — the *Our Father* or *Come Holy Spirit*
— but more frequently by a spontaneous prayer said by the
one who, on this occasion, is the prayer leader. Through this
prayer the participants remind each other that they are gathered
in the name of Jesus and that he is, therefore, in their midst.
Then follows a reading either from the scriptures or from
another book. Preferably, the participants know the text before-
hand. The person responsible for the prayer meeting may, in
a few words, give a comment on it.

Five or ten minutes of silence follow. It is a time for very
personal listening to God's word. Then, as the Spirit inspires
each one, there is the sharing of thoughts. Sometimes it is a
dialogue about things that have struck each one of the participants. But as I have experienced it in various parts of the
world, it more often becomes a direct response to the Lord.

Prayers of supplication, of thanksgiving, of praise, of sorrow
for past sins and trust in the Lord's mercy, in a sharing of
reflections and experiences, become almost always prayer of
vigilance. The very spontaneity fostered by this kind of prayer
does not so easily allow mere repetition and evasion.

One of the most important conditions for this style of prayer
is mutual trust. What is shared in these events can never
become an object of criticism or reproach. There will never be
a dispute or contradiction. The imperfection of our expressions
is fully accepted. Through the sharing by people of various
temperaments and charisms, even the most imperfect word
contributes to the whole picture. The mutual trust manifested
in this form of prayer creates a divine *milieu*. It builds community based on a living faith in one God.

3. *Various occasions for shared prayer*

The spontaneity of the meetings for shared prayer shows
its impact on the life of the participating families, friends and
groups. Not only in family meetings but on various other

occasions, they will spontaneously share their reflections on the joyful and sorrowful experiences of life. Together they will decipher the signs of God's presence in the concrete moment and event.

Morning and evening prayer, the evening examination of conscience, the prayer at mealtimes are all becoming again, in Christian families, spontaneous expressions which unite the members of the family much more in faith than a simple recitation of even a very beautiful formal prayer. In spontaneous prayer, nobody will try to produce classic literature; it is simply the expression of faith and vigilance for the Lord's coming.

In the life of the Church, the new liturgical legislation and the new spirit in this post-conciliar era allow and promote spontaneous shared prayers in various parts of the liturgy. I speak, of course, only of those occasions when, according to the present liturgical legislation, we can be spontaneous and creative. It is clear that our communal worship cannot be all sponeaneity and creativity. And it must never become anarchic.

(a) *The service of penance*

A number of episcopal conferences have proposed various models of the service of penance at the beginning of the Mass, and have made clear that they want these models to stimulate a greater variety and spontaneity on these occasions.

In the simplest model, the priest reminds us in his own words that we celebrate the Eucharist for the forgiveness of our sins, and that the more we are aware of our need for forgiveness and conversion, the greater will be the fruit of this celebration. Then follows an invitation to examine our conscience, usually on a specific and important point, in view of the particular liturgy or in view of the concrete situation of our life. The various prayers for the forgiveness of sins follow. It is desirable that not all of these should be formulated by the priest alone, that other participants should be allowed and encouraged to share their prayers for forgiveness, as reflected in their examination of conscience.

Communal celebrations of the sacrament of reconciliation, which are now not only allowed but desired by the supreme authority of the Church, lead to a deeper examination of conscience and a more profound sharing in sorrow for our sins and in our renewed purpose. Very important in these celebrations is the renewal of our commitment to be messengers of peace and reconciliation, and to show mercy because mercy is shown to us. All this should be a part of thanksgiving and praise for God's mercy, for the undeserved gift of our own peace and reconciliation.

(b) *Sharing meditation on the word of God*

What I have said about the common model of shared meditation can apply also to the liturgy after the readings. It is evident that, within the liturgy, any kind of debate is even more excluded than in shared prayer outside the liturgy. We all have our own way of receiving the word of God and treasuring it up in our hearts. This is prayer; it is a response. But it seems that we respond even better if, in our response, we share the gifts of the Spirit and our insights. I have often heard excellent homilies by the best preachers, and also have often assisted in shared meditation. And I think that a single person, even a very gifted priest, can seldom make such a contribution as is made by the sharing of our reflections on the word of God.

(c) *The profession of faith*

In the previous chapter I have given a few models that show how the community can make the profession of faith a meditation and a very intense prayer of faith and vigilance. I proposed only a few examples: faith in the dignity of all people, faith and solidarity, faith and joy, faith and freedom. There can be many more themes that manifest the dynamic nature of our faith towards a new life in Christ Jesus. Our profession of faith can tell us, for instance, much about peace, reconciliation, mercy and compassion, humility, generosity, purity of intention, sincerity and truthfulness with each other, and so on.

(d) *The prayer of the faithful*

Dialogue on the word of God or dialogue-homily leads naturally to spontaneous prayer. But even when there is no sharing of reflections on the readings, there should be communal participation in the prayer of the faithful. Two forms have often been explored. In one, the various groups meditate together before the liturgy, on what their prayer should be this day. The other is the immediate expression of the intentions and prayers of the participants.

Again it should be emphasized that nobody is expected to produce great literature. The style mirrors the freedom of the children of God expressing their concern, their joy, their need or their sorrow. In small communities I have seen that as the communicants put the altar bread on the paten at the offertory procession, each one also expresses his intention, his prayer of supplication, thanksgiving or praise.

(e) *Spontaneous thanksgiving after Communion*

Eucharist means literally thanksgiving. The Church favours the practice of allowing a time of sacred silence after Communion, when we render thanks to the Lord, rejoice in his presence, and meditate on how we can transform our life in the spirit of the Eucharist, to offer it as a sign of abiding gratitude to God. Then there can be a spontaneous sharing of thanksgiving. A number of the psalms came into being through such a kind of sharing, with the response of all the people, 'For your mercy is without end.'

Sharing in this prayer of thanksgiving, we receive inspiration and insight on how to live all our life — including our handicaps, our limitations and failures — in such a way as to render thanks to the Lord for all that he has done for us. We can indeed sing together a great song of joy and thanksgiving, even in view of our difficulties, because all of this is now redeemed and can enter into the praise which Christ offers to the Father in our name.

(f) *The divine office*

These few suggestions on how we should allow and foster spontaneity in the celebration of the Eucharist can also apply to the celebration of all the other sacraments. It is just not normal that in the liturgy there should be no place for a personal spontaneous expression. The divine office gives us occasions similar to the celebration of the Eucharist: reflection and its sharing after the reading, spontaneous prayer at the beginning or at the end, the petitions and the chorus of thanksgiving in which all people join.

✝ We ask you, Lord, to give to your Church the experience of a new pentecost. May all the languages, all the temperaments and charisms of all people unite in a great chorus to your praise.

Grant us a community of brothers and sisters who, with their deep faith and prayer, can strengthen our faith where it falls short.

Cleanse us, O Lord, and unite us in a joyous faith through which we can comfort the sufferers and support them in their faith.

Come, Holy Spirit, free us from closed minds, from isolation, from anguish and mistrust. Make us free for you, docile to your inspirations, so that all our life may become one voice, one outcry of joy: 'Abba, Father!'

Chapter 7

HOUSES OF PRAYER: SCHOOLS OF PRAYER

In a community in which people are gathered by faith, the whole of life becomes a school of prayer: that is, of the integration of all experiences and shared reflections in the adoration of God in spirit and truth. Whoever sees the relation between wholeness and holiness will do everything in his power to come to a true synthesis of faith, vigilance for the present opportunities, and praise of God.

Her divine Founder intended the Church to be a 'house of prayer' and a school of prayer for all nations and at all times. 'I will bring them to my holy mountain and fill them with joy in my house of prayer, for my house shall be called a house of prayer for all peoples' (Is 56:7).

For the Church as a whole and for all her various communities, the most serious question of conscience is whether she is truly that house of prayer in which all find joy and learn what it means to adore the Son of God and God the Father in an authentic way. In the New Testament, we see Jesus only once in holy wrath, and that is when he sees how unworthy the cult in the temple is. 'Scripture has it: my house shall be called a house of prayer, but you are turning it into a den of thieves' (Mt 21:13).

132

1. *New needs demand new efforts*

Each person, in each phase and situation of his life, has to learn again how to express himself or herself before God, and how to integrate a growing faith with actual life. The Church has entered into a new phase of her life, a new era, a secular age. Her faith remains always the same; yet in each age it has to be expressed in such a way that it becomes, for those living in that age, the very heart of life.

A movement that spreads all over the world and calls itself 'house of prayer' tries to respond to this particular need in our age. It aims at overcoming the crisis of faith. It is inspired by the conviction that true reconciliation and renewal have their vital centre in prayer. If this is true, then it does not suffice to exhort people to pray; there must also be offered schools of prayer, centres of spirituality adapted to the needs of our times, our age, our culture. After all, priests, religious and lay people are all learners in the field of faith and prayer.

In response to new needs and opportunities, numerous groups arose in almost all countries immediately after the Second Vatican Council. The best known in the English-speaking world are the prayer groups of the charismatic renewal, or the 'Catholic pentecostals'. They gather regularly and often create a very vital atmosphere of friendship. However, the 'house of prayer' movement is looking for greater intensity in prayer. Integration of faith and life goes deeper if those who pray together also share their daily life. I asked a young Jewish convert, a university student, what she had learned in a house of prayer after she had participated for two months. Her response was typical: 'I have seen what a true community of faith is'.

The houses of prayer have diverse forms, and this seems to be a necessity since their purpose is to provide a learning process that aims at bringing actual life into the experience of faith. As I have repeatedly stressed, the effort to deepen our knowledge of man and our life of prayer always has its centre in the growth

of the knowledge of God. People who participate are looking
not only for occasions and places to pray with others but for the
opportunity to share in an authentic experience of faith that
gives shape to their whole life.

The house of prayer movement follows the rationale of
Mahatma Ghandi. Before he began his great non-violent crusade
for the liberation and equality of all people, in South Africa and
later in India, he founded *ashrams,* which means houses of
prayer. He insisted that only those who come to full consciousness of their union with God can reach out to full consciousness
of the unity and brotherhood of all men. But he also knew that
one cannot come to a truthful awareness of his union with God
if he does not, at the same time, aim at unity, justice and
brotherhood among men.

I think that the house of prayer movement, as well as
charismatic renewal, has roots in the Second Vatican Council's
new emphasis on initiative, creativity and vigilance as fruits of a
life in the Spirit. The efforts for a renewal of prayer life are at
the very heart of the renewal of the Church and of reconciliation
of man with God and among ourselves.

In their greatest and best moments, the contemplative
communities of men and women were not an evasion or a
separation from life but an effort to be models of the synthesis
of love for God and love for neighbour, of prayer and community
life. The association of contemplative nuns in North America
wants to restore this best tradition. A number of contemplative
cloisters are moving in the same direction as the houses of prayer.
They, too, want their houses to be not only places in which
prayers are offered for all mankind but also schools of integration
of life and prayer, and places where other believers can join them
to deepen their life of faith.

About ten years ago I asked a number of contemplative
cloistered communities of men and women two questions: 1) Do
you think your communities could offer themselves as schools
of prayer for priests, active apostolic sisters and lay people?
2) Do you consider it a good idea to encourage members of

active religious communities, secular priests, and even lay people
to live in communities where the first aim is to find a way to
integrate prayer and life, and to form centres or schools of prayer
for today's people?

Most of my contemplative friends very humbly responded to
the first question that they did not think they were able to fulfil
such an important role in the existing form of their own style
of prayer life. But all emphatically encouraged the idea of
promoting this new type of house of prayer. Some expressed
quite plainly the hope that this would give new inspiration to
a renewal of their own communities.

2. *Different forms of houses of prayer*

A house of prayer is different from the traditional house for
retreats. It is not an operation for preaching to others or being
preached to, but rather a community of persons whose main
goal is to find for themselves a deep integrity in faith and prayer.
The emphasis is on sharing with others, learning together how
to see everything in the light of faith, and how to bring all life
home into the praise of the Creator and Redeemer.

At the present time houses of prayer are arising under
various names such as 'centre of spiritual renewal' or 'school of
faith'. The first initiative came from active congregations of
sisters who opened houses of prayer as integral parts of their
communities: first for themselves, and then also for young
women or other lay people who wanted to join them. There are
houses of prayer for men religious — fathers and brothers — and
also for secular priests, and a number of houses of prayer for
ecumenical groups of priests, ministers and lay people.

In Latin America and South Africa, many of the houses of
prayer have a spirituality similar to that of Ghandi's *ashrams*.
For them, contemplation of the Word Incarnate is preparation
for a deep and permanent commitment to the liberation of all
people. To my knowledge, almost all of the houses of prayer are

deeply sensitive to the poor and disadvantaged. This must be so if they promote a renewal of prayer in the prophetic traditions. But there must be concern not only for those who are poor in material goods but also for people who are disadvantaged because they have not found the spiritual dimension of their lives.

A number of houses of prayer offer opportunity for others to make their spiritual retreat. Usually it is a retreat directed by members of the house of prayer, with a guide on a one-to-one basis. The relationship is a person-to-person sharing of faith. But the decisive factor is the atmosphere of the whole community in which everyone's chief concern is to learn how to adore God in spirit and truth.

There are permanent houses of prayer and houses of prayer for certain periods of time. Most of the permanent houses are founded and supported by one or more active religious communities. A core group of from three to twelve members remain there for a year or sometimes longer. Someone who has a special charism may remain as animator for a considerable period of time or even for a lifetime. But nobody has the guarantee of a lifetime assignment. Such a community is not meant for people who are weary and want to flee from apostolic activity. Those who come must always be ready to return with new zeal to the active apostolic life. But whether one remains in the house of prayer or returns somewhere else, the main purpose will always be to help each community and the whole Church to become more and more what God promised: 'a house of prayer for all nations'.

Some of the permanent houses of prayer put the main emphasis on contemplation, and try to unite it with a spiritual theology as a way to synthesize meditative study of the word of God with discernment of the signs of the times.

Most of the houses of prayer have begun very soon to exercise an active ministry as schools of prayer for priests and lay people who stay with them for a certain time or come regularly for prayer meetings and orientation on how to find the synthesis ɔf life. In many of the houses, some of the members continue a professional activity, but in a way that guarantees enough time and energy for a deepened life of contemplation and prayer. What makes a house a house of prayer is the fact that all the members are united in a main purpose and are ready to sustain an ongoing effort to pray better and to look for a better synthesis of life and faith. Thus they guarantee for each participant a divine *milieu* conducive to prayer.

Probably more numerous than the permanent ones are the temporary houses of prayer. This form was initiated, with great creativity and success, by the Sisters Servants of the Immaculate Heart in Monroe, Michigan. About a hundred and forty sisters of their own congregation and of several other congregations, prepared themselves, through various meetings throughout the year, for the venture which took place in the summer of 1969. During those seven weeks, the sisters lived, in small groups of five to fifteen, in houses which, during the scholastic year, were occupied by teaching sisters.

At their disposal were a number of advisors, some priests and some members of contemplative communities, a brother who is also a psychologist and expert in Zen, a swami and a Rabbi who, besides being a psychologist, had special experience with a synagogue that follows the same trend as the house of prayer. All the groups met together several times and exchanged their experiences. The sisters called this summer experience the 'house of prayer experience', with the initials H O P E.

And indeed these initiatives are signs of hope. Many communities throughout the world have followed with similar efforts to provide times of renewal in depth. Repeatedly I have had the opportunity to preach retreats at the beginning, middle or end of such events, or simply to be present and participate for a certain time. Each time I have been deeply impressed by the spirit of joy and peace, and of readiness to return to the apostolate to become promoters in renewal of prayer life.

3. *Experiences and reflections*

For me and for many others, the strongest impression of houses of prayer has been the spiritual atmosphere of joy, peace, kindness, and a divine *milieu* that exercises an extraordinary influence on those who share this life. There are sometimes also different ideas and expectations about prayer — what it should be, the extent of silence, and so on. But even these differences in ideas can and often do become creative. As long as all are of one mind about finding a synthesis between love of God and love of neighbour, they will accept each other and search together for a viable synthesis.

Such a divine *milieu* often exercises a remarkable healing power. I know cases where persons who previously had been treated by psychotherapists for a long time with no discernable success have found perfect peace and a new harmony in such an atmosphere after only two or three weeks. Repeatedly, too, participants have told me that after about a week in such a divine environment, they could unwind, become free from haste and hurry, and thus could rejoice in the presence of God and find the meaning of silence as well as of shared prayer.

In many houses of prayer, one finds a good synthesis between creative freedom and creative fidelity. In the house of prayer, persons are bound together more by common goals and ideals than by a set of rules. While there is a clear expectation of the end in view, there is also space for spontaneity and creativity. These qualities are possible because the participants form a community of faith, and their trust in God engenders also mutual respect and trust.

Since a house of prayer means a community of persons gathered round the person of Christ, there is the highest appreciation of the word of God. They meditate personally and together on the word of God; they treasure it up in their hearts, and share their experiences in praise, thanksgiving and supplication. There is no preoccupation with producing good literature. There is an atmosphere of openness to the word of God and to the Spirit who works in all, through all and for all. Where the listening to the word of God in the scriptures is authentic, it always leads to vigilance, openness, and discernment.

A divine *milieu* of faith and thanksgiving frees one from pessimism, anguish and insecurity, and from temptation to bitter criticism. Everyone can see what the harvest of the Spirit is: 'love, joy, peace, patience, kindness, goodness, fidelity, gentleness and self-control' (Eph 5:22).

In a climate of mutual trust and respect, the revision of life receives new dimensions. A new sensitivity to God's gifts leads also to a greater sensitivity and sharpness of conscience. In the climate of mutual trust and trust in God, people become not only sincere with each other but also more sincere with themselves.

The houses of prayer seem to favour a spiritual atmosphere most appropriate for that approach to theology described in Chapter 3. The participants grow in the spirit of discernment. Often they find, almost naturally, the criteria for their choice of books, and thus theology transforms itself into doxology, into praise of God, joy, peace, pastoral zeal, better knowledge of man and his lofty vocation in Christ.

A sister who had a doctorate in theology and had been teaching many years said, after having participated twice for six weeks in a house of prayer, 'I have in this time learned more about what theology is than in all the years of my formation and teaching'. So I think the renewal of prayer promoted by the houses of prayer and by various other movements of renewal in prayer, allows the hope of a renewal of spiritual theology.

Thousands of people — religious, priests and lay people — have participated in the experience of houses of prayer. The increased spontaneity, the sharing in prayer and renewed sense of vigilance show their truth also in greater creativity regarding the apostolate. A person who has found his integration in prayer can do more for the evangelization of the world of today than can hundreds of restless activists and well-trained functionaries and administrators who lack spiritual experience of a deeper sort. In every epoch, the renewal of the apostolate goes hand in hand with an authentic life of prayer.

People who are moulded in their spirituality by the houses of prayer have begun to go to prisons as social workers. Some have inaugurated prayer groups for prisoners. Others have found an urgent need to visit the sick in hospitals and to pray with them; and still others have begun to visit lonely old people, to pray with them and help them in their needs.

One of the most urgent and truthful forms of apostolate is that of helping Christian families to discover their vocation to be a house of prayer and a school of faith. Experience of prayer groups in all the various movements — the charismatic renewal, houses of prayer and similar movements — has already made a great contribution to Christian families, and especially to the young who are seeking for an authentic religious experience. These groups want to find in the Church greater hope and make her 'a house of prayer that brings joy to all nations.'

In all this, however, we cannot see more than the first signs of a springtime. Everything depends on our readiness to unite our energies in this direction. The appeal to reconciliation, which Pope Paul offers for the holy year 1975, cannot bear its fruit if we do not give priority to the renewal in our life of prayer. Prayer is response to God who reconciles us and consolidates our commitment to reconciliation and peace among men.

✛   Father, you have created the earth for mankind and made it a dwelling place for your love. Wherever people are united in your name, and seek nothing more than to grow in the knowledge of your glory and your design for them, there is paradise.

We praise you for all the men and women, families and communities that, throughout history and around the earth, have been close to you and have, by their holy lives, taught and encouraged others to adore you. We thank you for each oasis where prayerful people live together or gather regularly to learn how to know you more intimately and to honour your name.

We thank you for the *ashrams* where Mahatma Ghandi and his friends attained that profound consciousness of their union with you that enabled them to consecrate themselves totally to the cause of freedom and unity for all people and all nations.

We praise you for those houses of prayer where we can experience your gracious presence and learn to be more alert to your coming in the daily events of our lives.

We implore you, Father, let all men and women find, sometime in their lives, a house of prayer that will enlighten and encourage them to make, of their own family or community, a school of prayer. And we ask you to bless all those who have dedicated themselves to the ministry of prayer.

Epilogue

A HOPE OR A DREAM?

The future of the Church and of the world depend, above all, on the response we give to the most striking signs of our times. The affluent society, with its quasi-religious trust in technological achievements, has not led to greater happiness or human growth. Criminality, violence, terrorism are rapidly increasing. Millions of people have become alcoholics and drug addicts. Air and water pollution is but the realistic symbol of a poisoned human *milieu*, distorted values, disturbed and manipulated public opinion, and sophisticated forms of exploitation of men's passions and their real or artificially created needs.

The ruthlessness with which a small, wealthy minority has exploited the material resources of our little planet, the rapid increase in the world's population, and the sharpened sensitivity to social and international justice impose on our society a responsibility for profound changes in itself. Futurologists speak of the unavoidable 'third revolution' if mankind is to have any hope of peace and humanness and to avoid an ecological catastrophe. This 'third revolution' requires a conversion to spiritual values, especially to altruism and simplicity. What behaviourism or psycho-analysis can offer us in view of the tremendous needs of the future is no more than a 'little mouse'. Certainly I am ready to take advantage of what the behavioural sciences can teach us; but we need wholly new dimensions and new energies.

142

I see signs of hope in the considerable portion of the youth of all nations who turn away from the idols of the materialistic, affluent societies with their mistaken dynamics towards ever greater material needs and increased consumption of material goods. Youth seeks spiritual experience: it wants to explore the inner space.

The great traditions of the contemplative religions of Asia, and a spiritual renewal in parts of the Islamic world offer us models that question our occidental fever for transforming our environment without knowing about our own human possibilities for growth and transformation. I do not mean that we should abdicate our mission to transform the world around us; but it should not be done in a way that leads to depletion and imbalance. Man has to discover again that his greatest and noblest task is to become more and more an image and likeness of God; and for that goal, all the energies of all people have to unite in creating 'a divine *milieu*' that mirrors and fosters man's lofty vocation to be co-creator with God and co-revealer of his goodness.

Thousands of the American and European young turn to Indian gurus or Asian Zen-masters, but far more gather in Taizé and other centres of spiritual renewal. The Church has a unique opportunity if she can read the signs of the times. Thailand, with its thirty-five million inhabitants has, according to official statistics, three hundred and fifty thousand Buddhist monks. Between ten and fifteen per cent are life-long monks; the others are youths who, for a certain number of months or years, live in the schools of contemplation with those monks who have chosen to be, for their whole lifetime, learners and teachers of humour, contemplation and compassion. For these contemplative Asian cultures and for decisive portions of the young everywhere, Christianity can be an incarnate, credible and attractive gospel when we find the way to integrate contemplation and the transformation of the world. The most needed event is that we all turn to Christ, the teacher and model of prayer.

In various parts of Asia there are being founded a number

of Christian *ashrams*, houses of prayer. Some follow the older models of the contemplative cloister; others are typically Asian forms of schools of faith, spiritual centres that practice and teach the integration of faith and life in prayer — or 'Christian contemplation', that is, contemplation in the Word Incarnate.

People shaped by the old Asian contemplative traditions do appreciate the achievements of the Christian Churches in education and social assistance; but if we have no more to offer than that, they pity us. Our credibility depends on our radical conversion to the gospel, with its emphasis on the prime importance of prayer as the synthesis of the knowledge of God and knowledge of man, of love of God and love of our neighbour. Here are the only forces that can bring about the 'third revolution'. Here are the chief healing powers that can prevent the frightening increase in the number of alcoholics, drug addicts, neurotics and psychotics.

The world of today needs, more than anything else, families and communities that, by their being, their witness and service, help mankind to seek first things first, to overcome the spiritual vacuum, to rejoice in the presence of the Lord, to be vigilant for the present opportunities.

✛ Lord, with your disciples we beseech you, 'teach us how to pray'. Teach us how to transform all our life into adoration of the Father 'in spirit and in truth'. Teach us how to pray as men and women of this new era that does not allow us the mediocrity or evasion of superficial devotions.

Lord, send forth your Spirit to help us become fully sincere in our prayer and in the shaping of our daily life and social commitments. Cleanse us from our sins, from selfishness and superficiality. Help us to progress in the knowledge that is eternal life, in 'knowing you who alone are truly God, and Jesus Christ whom you have sent'.

We believe that only through the undeserved gift of the Spirit can we come to truthful adoration of your name. When the Spirit dwells in us and we become docile to him, we can call you, in joy and in truth, 'Our Father'. But we know, too, through your revelation, that your abundant gifts and promises do not allow us to be lazy. You ask and make possible our creative co-operation.

Make us grateful, Lord; make us vigilant, so that each of us, our families and our communities, may join hands and energies to create the best possible conditions for the synthesis of faith and life, of prayer and service to our brethren, in this new epoch of human history.

AMEN.